SEEDS

SEEDS

A documentary play by

Annabel Soutar

TALONBOOKS

Talonbooks
P.O. Box 2076, Vancouver, British Columbia, Canada V6B 3S3
www.talonbooks.com

Typeset in Frutiger Serif
Printed and bound in Canada on 100% post-consumer recycled paper
Cover design by Marijke Friesen

Second printing: January 2014

Talonbooks gratefully acknowledges the financial support of the Canada Council for the Arts, the Government of Canada through the Canada Book Fund, and the Province of British Columbia through the British Columbia Arts Council and the Book Publishing Tax Credit.

Library and Archives Canada Cataloguing in Publication

Soutar, Annabel, 1971–

Seeds / Annabel Soutar.

Issued also in electronic format.

ISBN 978-0-88922-701-9

1. Schmeiser, Percy, 1931– —Trials, litigation, etc.—Drama. 2. Monsanto Canada Inc.—Trials, litigation, etc.—Drama. I. Title.

PS8637.O94S44 2012   C812'.6   C2012-904303-6

For my two seeds,
Ella and Beatrice

ACKNOWLEDGEMENTS

Writing *Seeds* was a profoundly collaborative effort from start to finish. Every character in the play is a real person and many of them spoke to me directly in lengthy interviews and generously agreed to have their words included verbatim in this play. I want to especially thank Terry Zakreski and Dr. Illimar Altosaar for continuing to provide me with context and clarification while I was working on final drafts of the script.

I am grateful to the cast and artistic team who worked on an earlier version of *Seeds* with me in 2005: Andreas Apergis, Jonas Bouchard, Ana Cappelluto, Chip Chuipka, Richard Cliff, Alex Ivanovici, Greg Kramer, Alexander MacSween, Joel Miller, Jennifer Morehouse, and Julie Tamiko Manning.

This version of the text was workshopped extensively in Montreal before its Toronto premiere in February 2012. I will forever be indebted to the actors who boldly confronted and helped me shape the script during that time: Bruce Dinsmore, Mariah Inger, Alex Ivanovici, Tanja Jacobs, Cary Lawrence, Eric Peterson, and Liisa Repo-Martell. Thank you also to Ana Cappelluto, Mitchell Cushman, Chad Dembski, Richard Feren, Julie Fox, Elysha Poirier, Camille Robillard, Angeline St. Amour, and Eric Savory for their hard work and insight during the workshop process.

To my colleagues at Porte Parole – Jean-François Garneau, Annie Perron, and Joël Richard – your determination made this version of *Seeds* possible. Thank you also to Porte Parole's board of directors, past and present, for supporting this work in infinite ways. Special thanks to Farès Khoury for believing in me for so long.

I am grateful to Monica Esteves and Hilary Green at Crow's Theatre for taking a chance on producing *Seeds*.

Thank you to Chris Abraham, whose brilliant fingerprints are all over this script and without whom this new version of *Seeds* may not have seen the light of day.

Thank you to my family, who has been behind me throughout this long process and who knows intimately what I have given up to write *Seeds*: my parents, Ian and Helgi; my brothers, James and Adam; my sister-in-law, Abby; and my two daughters, Ella and Beatrice.

Finally, thank you to my husband, Alex Ivanovici, whose remarkable talent for living poetically inspires and sustains me every day.

Development of *Seeds* has been generously supported by the Conseil des arts et des lettres du Québec, the Canada Council for the Arts, the Conseil des arts de Montréal, the Hexagram-Concordia Centre for Research-Creation in Media Arts and Technologies, York University, and Playwrights' Workshop Montréal.

A co-production by Crow's Theatre (Toronto) and Porte Parole (Montreal), *Seeds* premiered on February 22, 2012, at the Young Centre for the Performing Arts in Toronto, Ontario, with the following cast and crew:

Bruce Dinsmore
Carlyle Moritz, Tony Creber, Dr. Keith Downey, John Honderich, Dr. Vandana Shiva, Retired Bruno Farmer 1, Dr. Barry Commoner

Mariah Inger
Nadège Adam, James Vancha, Lyle Friesen, Morris Hofmann, Wesley Niebrugge, Zita Maier, Moritz's Wife, Johannesburg Radio Interviewer

Alex Ivanovici
Terry Zakreski, Dr. Illimar Altosaar, Old Indian Farmer, Playwright's Husband, Jeff Hoiness

Tanja Jacobs
Louise Schmeiser, Roger Hughes, Maude Barlow, Dr. Ann Clark, Sister Catherine Fairbairn, Retired Bruno Farmer 2

Cary Lawrence
Trish Jordan, Don Todd, Dr. Rene Van Acker, Mary-Deanne Shears, Shop Clerk, Bruno Farmer's Wife

Eric Peterson
Percy Schmeiser

Liisa Repo-Martell
Playwright, Supreme Court Justices

❋

Chris Abraham
Director

Ana Cappelluto
Lighting Design

Mitchell Cushman
Assistant Director

Richard Feren
Sound Design and Music Composition

Julie Fox
Set and Costume Design

Elysha Poirier
Video and Projection / Media Design

CHARACTERS
(in order of appearance)

Playwright: a Montreal-based documentary theatre creator, thirties

Lab Technicians: various, played by five different actors

Trish Jordan: public relations director for Monsanto Canada, thirties

Percy Schmeiser: a Saskatchewan farmer, early seventies

Louise Schmeiser: Percy's wife, early seventies

Terry Zakreski: Percy's lawyer, thirties

Roger Hughes: lawyer for Monsanto, sixties

Carlyle Moritz: Percy's farm assistant, early thirties

Tony Creber: lawyer for BIOTECanada, early fifties

Nadège Adam: spokesperson for the Council of Canadians, late twenties

Maude Barlow: national chairperson for the Council of Canadians, fifties

Don Todd: private investigator for Robinson Investigations, age unknown

James Vancha: associate manager of intellectual property, Monsanto, age unknown

Dr. Keith Downey: seed scientist, seventies

Dr. Ann Clark: associate professor of plant agriculture, University of Guelph, Ontario, fifties

Lyle Friesen: weed scientist at the University of Manitoba, late thirties

Dr. Rene Van Acker: weed scientist at the University of Manitoba, forties

Morris Hofmann: assistant manager of farm supplies, Humboldt Flour Mill, sixties

Dr. Illimar Altosaar: professor of biochemistry, microbiology, and immunology, University of Ottawa, male, fifties

Wesley Niebrugge: farmer and fuel station attendant, forties

Sister Catherine Fairbairn: nun, member of the Grey Sisters of the Immaculate Conception, early sixties

John Honderich: publisher of the *Toronto Star*, sixties

Mary-Deanne Shears: managing editor at the *Toronto Star*

Dr. Vandana Shiva: Indian seed scientist and activist, fifties

Old Indian Farmer: eighties

Zita Maier: a reporter for the *Prairie Messenger*, late sixties

Playwright's Husband: thirties

Dr. Barry Commoner: senior scientist at the Center for the Biology of Natural Systems at Queens College, City University of New York, eighties

Jeff Hoiness: Saskatchewan farmer and representative of the Canadian Canola Growers Association, fifties

Moritz's Wife: early thirties

Shop Clerk in Bruno, Saskatchewan: female, twenties

Johannesburg Radio Interviewer: female, age unknown

Retired Farmer 1: seventies

Retired Farmer 2: seventies

Supreme Court Justices: performed by the actress playing the playwright

Bruno Farmer's Wife: sixties

Other characters, played by various actors: Francis Crick, Restaurant Maître d', Nadège's Colleague, Court Clerk, Interjecting Voice, Ultrasound Technician

A NOTE ON THE TEXT

The text of *Seeds* is made up primarily of verbatim language from interview testimony, court trial transcript, and newspaper articles. Priority should be given, therefore, to respecting the syntactical idiosyncrasies (however awkward) of each character.

The stage directions in this version of *Seeds* are based on Chris Abraham's vision that every actor should be present onstage at all times. Entrances and exits refer to moments when characters leave the central action of a scene, but remain somewhere in the stage picture. Interjections made by characters who are not in a scene are facilitated by their presence onstage throughout the play.

Abraham and set designer Julie Fox conceived of the *Seeds* stage environment as a laboratory and of the actors as scientists and lab technicians. Reference is therefore made to the actors in this version as "lab technicians" when they are helping the playwright narrate her story.

Abraham also made use of projected text, video, and still images to narrate *Seeds*. Some of these projections have been referred to here to suggest how they can support the action onstage.

The epilogue in this version of the text includes information about events in the summer of 2012 relating to the global debate about genetically modified seeds. This information should be modified in future productions of the play to describe events that are current at the time of presentation and relevant to the present-day audience.

PROLOGUE

PROJECTION (text):
Life?

The LAB TECHNICIANS conduct formal interviews with the audience about the definition of life. The interviews, which are mic'd and projected live onto the onstage screens, are performed as if the LAB TECHNICIANS are gathering samples for work in their lab.

The interviews conclude.

The PLAYWRIGHT addresses the audience. She is visibly pregnant.

PLAYWRIGHT:
So, life ... Well, let me start by saying ... life: a living thing, an *organism*, is defined scientifically by its ability to reproduce. For centuries, scientists observed this ... this ... this ... this ...

LAB TECHNICIAN 1:
This phenomenon.

PLAYWRIGHT:
... this ... *phenomenon* ... without knowing exactly how living organisms passed down their inherited traits from one generation to the next. They had always understood inheritance to be a kind of storytelling in which life relayed a biological narrative to its offspring, but they couldn't detect precisely how that story was being told.

In the early twentieth century, however, biologists finally discovered a ... a ...

LAB TECHNICIAN 2:
A cellular agent.

PLAYWRIGHT:
... a ... cellular *agent* ... one that appeared to record and to *transmit* life's genetic narrative. Locked inside the nucleus of the living cell, they identified a long sequence of different combinations of four nucleotides:

LAB TECHNICIAN 3:
Adenine, cytosine, guanine, and thymine. A, C, G, and T.

PLAYWRIGHT:
They called this sequence ...

LAB TECHNICIAN 1:
Deoxyribonucleic acid.

PLAYWRIGHT:
... or ...

LAB TECHNICIAN 4:
DNA.

PLAYWRIGHT:
... and declared it to be the most elemental organic alphabet. ACGT: these four simple letters could spell out the entire biological story of life.

So ... *life?* I have been working for a long while on this story about life ... But whenever I try to arrive at a final version of this story, I find that along the way something has ... shifted ... and I can no longer finish it.

So, I'd like to begin this evening in a spirit of ... huuulllty ... by saying that ...

JORDAN:
(*interrupting*) One thing we know for sure: DNA holds the key to life.

The recorded transcript of a Monsanto television ad plays: "As a farmer, you believe. You believe in every acre, in every crop, in hard work and commitment. You believe in the future of farming, and the vast opportunities that lie ahead.

And you believe in the yields of tomorrow ... and providing for our growing planet, generation after generation. We believe ... in you. And putting the best tools and technologies into your hands, so together we can double corn, soya bean, and cotton yields by 2030 through improved agronomic practices, advances in breeding better seeds, and the introduction of innovative biotechnology traits. And we believe you can produce more while using one-third less resources, by planting seeds that use less energy and water, and work side by side to ensure growth for a better world, today and tomorrow. By the year 2050, there will be nine billion people on Earth who will want a higher standard of living and a need for the crops you provide."

ACT ONE

SCENE 1

PERCY SCHMEISER enters. He speaks to the PLAYWRIGHT in interview.

PERCY:
This is the famous Field Number 2, right here, where it all first happened. I have two miles of land going that way, and a mile going that way. The field actually starts right by these power poles; that's where your actual field starts – your *ownership*.

PLAYWRIGHT:
Percy Schmeiser, farmer, at his home in Bruno, Saskatchewan.

PERCY:
To me, land – this land – represents life. And if I look back at this particular, uh, parcel of land ... this land, just what we see here, and I look back at how my father worked to clear it (this used to be almost solid bushland) and when I took it over ... the *time* that my wife, Louise, and I spent picking stumps and stones and workin' to get that land to what it is now, you see, to bring it so that it can produce crops ... So, the land becomes so part of you, you know? So, a person has a lot of mixed emotions, um ...

Pause.

Now, especially when all of a sudden you can't grow a crop ... your choice is taken away, our property is taken away from us against our wishes ...

JORDAN:
This is a pretty simplistic case: we, Monsanto, have a valid patent on something – a patent that was granted to us by the Canadian

Patent Office. This guy had our patented technology. He *knew* he had it, and he *used* it.

PROJECTION (text):
Trish Jordan, public relations director,
Monsanto Canada, Winnipeg

JORDAN:
So, whether you're a *musician* or a *playwright* or *whatever* – just use any other analogy you want – if you come up with some innovative product and it's *your idea*, right, and that product can gain you value – which is what most businesses are interested in, right, because that's what they do – then it's incumbent on them to say, well, "How do we share in the value of this technology and also capture some of that value back for us, and be rewarded for the investment that we have made?"

PLAYWRIGHT:
Trish Jordan initially refused to testify for this documentary when contacted in the fall of 2003. She then reluctantly agreed to an interview one month later when assured that the said documentary would be a ...

JORDAN:
A *balanced* ...

PLAYWRIGHT:
... a balanced portrait of the Monsanto–Schmeiser conflict.

JORDAN:
Monsanto provides a valuable technology. We have more than thirty thousand farmers in western Canada who have used this technology, right, by *choice*. And what we have heard over and over and over again from farmers is: "Hey! You know, I want to try this technology; I ... I like this technology ... um, I understand the terms and conditions of using it, and I'm willing to pay for access to this technology. But you know what? If I'm going to pay for this technology, then I expect everybody to play by the same rules." And this is just about one case, one individual, who in our mind wasn't playing by the rules.

SCENE 2

PROJECTION (image): A September 1998 news article from the Western Producer

LAB TECHNICIAN 1:
A Saskatchewan farmer is the target of the first lawsuit aimed at protecting genetically engineered plants in Canada.

A phone starts ringing.

PLAYWRIGHT:
The first newspaper article ever written about the Monsanto–Schmeiser legal battle was published in the *Western Producer* newspaper in September 1998. Monsanto Canada had already filed their lawsuit a month before that, alleging that Percy Schmeiser of Bruno, Saskatchewan, grew its genetically modified canola without a licence.

The phone stops ringing.

LAB TECHNICIAN 1:
Schmeiser did not respond to a telephone request for an interview.

JORDAN:
In the end, the case may not make it to court.

LAB TECHNICIAN 1:
... said a representative of Monsanto Canada.

JORDAN:
We're hoping we can resolve it without it going that way.

PROJECTION, on another screen (text):
Five years later: Bruno, Saskatchewan

A telephone is ringing in the present day. The sound of the ring should be different from the ringing phone in the flashback we have just seen.

PERCY:
Leave them on! Leave them on! This is a farmhouse.

PLAYWRIGHT:
They're really dirty though ...

She keeps her boots on. LOUISE enters.

LOUISE:
Percy, it's another call for you.

PERCY:
Tell them I'm busy. (*introducing the PLAYWRIGHT to LOUISE*) My wife, Louise.

PLAYWRIGHT:
Hello. Nice to meet you.

LOUISE:
How do you do?

PERCY:
We met in Ottawa. You're based in Ottawa, aren't you?

PLAYWRIGHT:
Montreal.

LOUISE exits to answer the phone. PERCY leads PLAYWRIGHT into his dining room.

PERCY:
Montreal! I think you told me that. (*chuckles*) Here, let me put your coat somewhere ... just head on in there.

PERCY exits.

PLAYWRIGHT:

Five years after Monsanto launched its legal case against Percy Schmeiser, I went to visit Percy and Louise Schmeiser at their farm in Bruno, Saskatchewan.

PERCY re-enters.

PERCY:

Sit there if you want ... I'm going to be over here. I just gotta put some of these boxes away ... I was doing some paperwork earlier ...

LOUISE enters.

PLAYWRIGHT:

Take your time ...

LOUISE:

Would you care for a cup of tea or coffee?

PLAYWRIGHT:

(*gesturing to her belly*) No, thank you. I'm trying not to drink caffeine.

LOUISE:

Oh my goodness. I didn't notice before!

PERCY:

Well, look at that.

LOUISE:

How far along are you?

PLAYWRIGHT:

(*to audience*) I was only four months at the time.

LOUISE:

Well, I can hardly tell. You're so tiny.

PERCY:

Can we get you some juice then?

PLAYWRIGHT:
Just a glass of water, thank you.

LOUISE:
Would you like ice in your water or no ice?

PLAYWRIGHT:
No ice, thank you.

LOUISE:
No, I don't care for ice either.

> *LOUISE leaves to get the water. PERCY is still clearing off the dining room table.*

PLAYWRIGHT:
Bruno is a small town about 90 kilometres northeast of Saskatoon. Before it became known as the epicentre of the infamous Monsanto v. Schmeiser case, it would have simply been described as a small but successful farming community settled by German and Ukrainian immigrants in the late nineteenth century.

> *LOUISE has re-entered and is wiping the table before setting down the glass of water.*

PERCY:
Louise has been busy cleaning. We had a bunch of the kids home over the weekend, and the grandkids, so you can imagine the disaster!

LOUISE:
I haven't cleaned my little grandchildren's finger marks off the table yet.

PERCY:
I can see them. Yeah. (*chuckles*)

LOUISE:
Aw, we all made 'em when we were little. When we all get together, it's twenty-six or twenty-seven, so you can imagine ...

PERCY:
    They come and go: a bed and breakfast!

    PERCY exits.

LOUISE:
    It's a lot, you know? The cooking and the cleaning up afterward.
    But you're glad when you hear they do want to come home,
    because when you hear of some families where their kids don't
    want to come home, it's kinda sad. You know, you gotta look at
    the two sides.

PLAYWRIGHT:
    Louise and Percy have five children and fifteen grandchildren.

LOUISE:
    Will this be your first?

PLAYWRIGHT:
    No, I have a sixteen-month-old daughter back in Montreal.

LOUISE:
    Oh, she must miss you. And you make movies?

    PERCY enters.

PLAYWRIGHT:
    No, theatre actually ... documentary theatre. I record what
    people say, and then I pass their words to actors who perform
    that language as the script of a play.

LOUISE:
    Oh my!

PLAYWRIGHT:
    Yeah. I find that people's spoken words are kind of like
    fingerprints.

    LOUISE smiles.

PERCY:
Well, we better get at this before I get more phone calls.
(*chuckles*)

A phone rings.

LOUISE:
Oh dear ...

LOUISE exits.

*The PLAYWRIGHT quickly gathers her notes with
prepared questions and puts her tape recorder close to
PERCY.*

PLAYWRIGHT:
Okay, are you ready?

PERCY:
Oh, I'm ready.

PLAYWRIGHT:
Um, when was the first time you heard of genetically modified
canola?

PERCY:
One day back in 1998, I get a phone call from the post office. I
had just come in from the farm – it was around suppertime –
and the lady said, "Percy, there's a mail parcel here for you." So, I
said, "Okay, after supper I'll come get it." So, I don't think I even
opened it after I brought it home. It was, you know, a letter, a
larger letter. And I don't think I even opened it that night – I was
tired. And when I came home the next day, I think it drizzled or
something and we couldn't cut, and I opened it and I look at it,
and I read it, you know, "patent infringement," you know? And
they said that I got thirty days to disclaim against it. It was called
a "statement of claim" in the judicial court of Saskatchewan, or
somethin' like that. So, anyway, a couple days, (*chuckles*) I still
didn't pay much attention to it because it didn't sink in. (*LOUISE
enters with a cup of coffee for PERCY.*) And a couple of days later,
Louise said:

LOUISE:

You know, I'm lookin' at this. You better go when you're in Humboldt to see the lawyer.

PERCY:

A lawyer I had for the farm, you know, to do the paperwork. So, I said okay. I took it along, and he looked at it and two minutes later he said – I'll never forget the words – he says, "Percy, I think you are in trouble. You gotta get yourself a *patent* lawyer."

TERRY ZAKRESKI enters.

ZAKRESKI:

One month after he received the statement of claim in the mail, Monsanto accused him of it – in the papers, in the *Western Producer* newspaper.

PLAYWRIGHT:

The patent lawyer that Percy found in Saskatoon was Terry Zakreski.

ZAKRESKI:

That's the first public volley fired. They never went out to his farm and took the time to deal with him. They sued first and asked questions later ... and they shouldn't have gone down that road.

PLAYWRIGHT:

Terry Zakreski told me that Percy was well known in his community, an active figure in Bruno municipal politics, and a long-time canola farmer and seed developer.

(*to ZAKRESKI*) Do you remember your first meeting with Percy?

ZAKRESKI:

Yeah, I remember our first meeting quite well. We hit it off instantly. It was the start of a great professional relationship between the two of us. I was struck by his story and I thought that he had a good case. And I thought I could do a lot for him.

PLAYWRIGHT:

Zakreski was young, but he walked with an unusual gait. I found out later that he had multiple sclerosis. Although he took care not to divulge confidential information about Percy to me, I could see that he cared deeply about the case and about his client.

ZAKRESKI:

Monsanto was accusing Percy of going out and buying pirated seed or bootleg seed and using that seed to plant his fields. And Percy was *so* adamant, *so* strong ... there was no way he would go out and do something like that. So, that's what the case was about at first: somebody being accused of something they didn't do.

Shift back to interview with PERCY.

PERCY:

You know, it might be best if we continue this in the field before it gets dark. It'll give you the lay of the land a bit ...

PLAYWRIGHT:

That would be great.

PERCY:

Louise! We're goin' out to the field now!

LOUISE:

All right!

PERCY:

(*as they put their coats on*) See, I have no problem if a seed company develops a seed, a seed that they don't want the farmer to sell to his neighbour. I have no problem with that. But to say you can't use the seed the next year that's left over from your crop? That's bad enough. But then to say that when the seed blows onto *my land*, against my wishes, and then to say you're not allowed to use your own seed? Well, that's gone too far. We'll take the half-ton. Louise!

LOUISE:

Yeah?!

PERCY:
We're taking the half-ton!

LOUISE:
Okay!

They get into the truck.

PERCY:
You can just keep asking me questions. I don't care if it's personal questions or pointed questions. I've spoken to so many media people over the past five years. So, you just go ahead.

PLAYWRIGHT:
Terry told me about how Monsanto went to the press right after they sent you notice of their lawsuit. How did you feel about the way they took the case public?

PERCY:
Well, it was very upsetting to me to all of a sudden see my name in the paper – that I *maybe* stole some seed. But you gotta remember: being in government and public life, I knew how corporations work, huhn? The first thing they try to do is discredit a person in public. People would come to me ... my neighbours ... and say, "Percy, you had to have done something wrong. A big company wouldn't come after you if you hadn't done something wrong." So, that's what I had to overcome in those initial years; I had to try to overcome that, you see?

ZAKRESKI:
Monsanto never dreamed that Percy would contest it; they thought that we would just give in and settle out of court. See, they just wanted a public example made – they just wanted the public to *know* that their patent rights were paramount, and that farmers better respect the patent, or Monsanto will come after you.

SCENE 3

A Saskatoon courtroom, June 5, 2000. ROGER HUGHES
appears and immediately gets to work launching the lawsuit.

HUGHES:

This is an action for patent infringement. The plaintiff, Monsanto
Company, owns a patent that pertains to a gene, which, when
incorporated into a crop – in this case canola – renders it tolerant
to a very powerful herbicide called Roundup.

PLAYWRIGHT:

Monsanto's chief council was a high-profile Toronto patent
lawyer named Roger Hughes.

HUGHES:

Roundup herbicide enables a farmer to spray a field, kill all the
weeds in the field, yet have the canola crop exist. That's the
theory of the patent.

PLAYWRIGHT:

Roger Hughes is the author of several textbooks on Canadian
patent law and a member of the Queen's Council. He is currently
an Ontario federal court judge.

HUGHES:

The canola into which this gene is incorporated reproduces itself;
therefore, if a farmer grows a crop and he retains the seeds, he
can subsequently grow crops that inherit this tendency. So,
Monsanto, in order to prevent that from happening, requires any
farmer who acquires the seed to sign what's called a Technology
Use Agreement, TUA, whereby the farmer undertakes *not* to
retain or sell or distribute the seeds to other people.

PLAYWRIGHT:

I called Mr. Hughes several times to get an interview about
the case.

HUGHES:

The manner in which Monsanto deals with this product requires that it continually monitor farmers who are suspected of acquiring the seed by other means without signing a contract – a process that is sometimes called brown bagging. Percy Schmeiser, the defendant, was one person who was subjected to this monitoring.

PLAYWRIGHT:

When I finally got him on the phone, he refused to be interviewed. I told him that Percy's lawyer, Terry Zakreski, had already spoken to me, to which he retorted:

HUGHES:

Any lawyer who accepts to comment publicly about an ongoing lawsuit is not fit to defend the honour of his profession.

HUGHES directs his last comment toward ZAKRESKI, who absorbs it as he prepares to present his case at trial.

PLAYWRIGHT:

I asked him how I could possibly tell the whole story if he wouldn't speak to me.

HUGHES:

Read the court transcripts.

PLAYWRIGHT:

I did. I paid several hundred dollars to get hard copies of the federal court transcripts of Monsanto v. Schmeiser. I remember picking them up at the post office in Montreal and stuffing them into the bottom of my baby stroller – four massive binders containing more than thirteen hundred pages. These transcripts are what you are hearing verbatim right now.

ZAKRESKI:

My Lord, my client is, and always has been, a conventional canola grower. He did not deliberately plant Roundup Ready canola seeds on his land. Now, I think it is important to point out right away that the patent that the plaintiffs rely upon is a patent for a *gene*, not a canola plant, and not a canola seed. It is our position that this gene is like a genie that's out of the bottle, and it has spread itself around the environment unchecked. And it is a *contaminant* that once unleashed into the environment cannot be controlled. And we call this a "contaminant," by the way, My Lord. The presence of this gene on Mr. Schmeiser's land is a contamination, and Mr. Schmeiser has a rational explanation for how this canola seed, with this gene in it, got on his property.

Back in PERCY's field.

PLAYWRIGHT:
Did you ever imagine in that moment that it would become such a big case?

PERCY:
Never. Never. Never. I just thought it would be thrown out – that it was a false claim. But the realization within a year – well, not even a year – after harvest, when I had more time to check, and *read* … You know, there were thirty-odd things in the thing of the patent that they had. Then I realized that there was such a thing as a *patent* on a *gene* inside the canola *seed*. That made it more complicated.

PERCY picks up some dirt from his field and rubs it between his hands.

Did you know that there's thousands of other genes in a seed? They just patented one. What gives them the right to claim ownership over all those other genes in the seed?

He brushes the dirt off his hands.

You should come back here in summertime; it's beautiful with the rolling green hills and the yellow canola …

SCENE 4

PLAYWRIGHT:

Before I started work on this project, I really didn't know exactly what a gene was and how it worked. But I realized pretty quickly that if I wanted to understand Monsanto's patent claims, I had to take a crash course in microbiology.

I gathered from some quick online research that the word "gene" was first used in the early twentieth century. But the term entered popular culture in 1953 when two molecular biologists named James Watson and Francis Crick announced their famous double helix theory of DNA.

FRANCIS CRICK:

DNA cracks the code of life!

PLAYWRIGHT:

They described the totality of human DNA – the human genome – as a precious manual written in As, Cs, Gs, and Ts, coiled inside the cell nucleus – a manual with precise instructions about whether an organism will evolve into a human or into a canola plant. This manual contains twenty-three little books that we call chromosomes – one-half passed down to us by our mothers and one-half by our fathers. These little books contain chapters called *genes* – that give specific instructions to the cell about how to build proteins in the living organism.

Now, imagine being able to precisely insert new letters into individual sentences in these books. This is exactly what GMO technology is attempting to do: essentially rewrite the molecular story and give new instructions to the organism about what kind of properties it should have – as in the case of GMO canola, where Monsanto inserts a gene into the plant's DNA that tells its cells to become resistant to the herbicide Roundup.

When you really think about it, the idea that human beings have figured out how to do this is quite astounding. When Percy was first sued by Monsanto in 1998, the Roundup Ready system was already a huge success with farmers because they no longer had to manually weed their fields. They just spray their whole field with this chemical and everything dies but your canola crop.

SCENE 5

ZAKRESKI examines PERCY in court.

ZAKRESKI:
Mr. Schmeiser, when did you first notice Roundup-resistant canola growing on your property?

PERCY:
The first time would have been in the end of June, first part of July, somewheres in there, just before flowering season 1997.

ZAKRESKI:
And how did you discover it?

PERCY:
I have a practice to spray Roundup around the power poles and the ditches alongside my land, to keep weeds from growing beside my property. And after spraying them that summer, I noticed that there was canola plants that did not die.

ZAKRESKI:
Did you have any assistance in carrying out this spraying operation?

> *CARLYLE MORITZ enters. We see him applying chemical to a field with a hand-held sprayer.*

PERCY:
Yes. My hired man helped me.

ZAKRESKI:
And what is your hired hand's name?

PERCY:
Carlyle Moritz.

> *Shift back to PLAYWRIGHT interviewing PERCY in his field.*

PERCY:

After Carlyle and I did the spray test, there was a plant here, a plant there; it was growing in clumps, thicker close to the road and then thinner as you went into the field. That told me it had to come from seed *blown* from somewheres. When we were doing research for the trial, Terry and I found out that another one of my neighbours in 1997 had hauled Monsanto's GMO canola past my land, and he admitted his tarp had broken and it was flapping in the wind, and he admitted he had lost some of his GMO canola seed along my land because my land is along the main road ... this road here is the main road leading to the crushing plant. But he didn't say anything to anybody at the time. So, *then* I knew how it got into my field.

> *JORDAN, in interview, interrupts to retell this story from her perspective.*

JORDAN:

So, Mr. Schmeiser tells the story about how he thinks this happened and how he *discovered* Roundup Ready canola in his field, right? So, from Monsanto's perspective? We don't think that story ever took place; we think that's a complete fabrication. But that's okay; he told it in a court of law. Here it is, his story: in 1997, Mr. Schmeiser went out and sprayed Roundup around his power poles, and some of the canola there survived. So, he *sprayed* three acres; this is what he testified to at trial. He said:

PERCY:

I'm gonna do this little experiment.

JORDAN:

"Cuz this is strange to me, and I don't understand why if I sprayed with Roundup, you know, I shouldn't have canola here." Well, first of all, I don't know a farmer in his right mind who would spray a canola field with Roundup, knowing that he's growing conventional canola – cuz you're gonna *kill* it. (*laughs*) Right? That's what it's designed to do, but ...

PERCY:

That's okay.

JORDAN:
"That's okay." So, he sprayed three acres. Sixty percent survived,
forty percent died. So, *then* he should have – well, I won't say
what he should have done – let's go with the story that he told.
So, then what did he do? Then he *harvested* whatever seed
survived and planted it in the fields the following year, knowing
he didn't want it there. He says he didn't know anything about
Roundup Ready canola; he "didn't want it there." He sprayed it
with Roundup; whatever survived obviously should be Roundup
resistant! I mean, there's no other explanation!

JORDAN exits.

23

SCENE 6

*TONY CREBER in interview with the PLAYWRIGHT at the
entrance to an Ottawa restaurant while they wait for a table.*

CREBER:
Uh (*small laugh*) believe it or not, I ... I believe in *fairness.*

PLAYWRIGHT:
I went to speak to a lawyer in Ottawa to see how other legal
experts viewed the case.

CREBER:
And I assume you believe in fairness, too. Right? But, any good
author has – I won't call it "literary licence," but there's a
selection of the pertinent facts, okay? So, I guess the question
is ... (*laughs softly*) Because there's the pure facts, which are fine.
There's the interpretation of those facts. And then there's the
selection of which facts are presented. We could end up with a
wildly different interpretation here, depending ... So, I'll try to
keep what *I'm* saying as purely factual and try to avoid too much
editorializing, because that's where I'm on "nervousness ground,"
for want of a better term.

PLAYWRIGHT:
Tony Creber is a lawyer for BIOTECanada, a lobby group
representing the interests of the biotech industry.

CREBER:
That's true. That's a fact. But there's one caveat I want to raise as a
concern before we go on, and that's that there are some ... what
I'll call "credibility issues" in this case. And just legally, if you say
something in court, there's privilege to what you say in court.
But *here* ... You see what I'm saying?

PLAYWRIGHT:
Not exactly.

CREBER:
Libel laws?

PLAYWRIGHT:
Okay.

CREBER:
Truth is a defence in court. But *here?*

Pause.

PLAYWRIGHT:
Um ... are there particular questions you would prefer me *not* to ask you?

CREBER:
(*lowers voice*) Well, no. You can ask me about it. Just *some* of Mr. Schmeiser's testimony in this case ... I just want to be a little careful. And I recommend that you also be careful about it. (*laughs*) Free advice.

MAÎTRE D':
Madame, Monsieur, your table is ready.

SCENE 7

A Saskatoon courtroom. ROGER HUGHES, counsel for
Monsanto, cross-examines PERCY.

HUGHES:
Now, Mr. Schmeiser, when you went back and saw that
60 percent of this Roundup Ready canola was still there after
you sprayed, you were surprised?

PERCY:
I was surprised because I had not seen it before.

HUGHES:
Okay. Did you take any photos?

PERCY:
No.

HUGHES:
Did you write it in your notebook?

PERCY:
No, I did not.

HUGHES:
So, it wasn't of any importance?

Pause.

PERCY:
No.

HUGHES:
Did you tell anyone about this?

PERCY:

No, I did not, and I had no reason to.

HUGHES:

You didn't have a consultant come down and take a look at this unusual circumstance that you saw?

PERCY:

No, and there was a reason for that, being that I had farmed canola for fifty years. I felt with the experience I had – that didn't even cross ...

HUGHES:

Did you consider it to be a *contamination*?

Pause.

PERCY:

Well, I knew there was canola in my field that did not die from Roundup, and I think that's maybe why I, to answer your question – I'm just thinking back here ...

HUGHES:

We're hoping you'll get to the answer, Mr. Schmeiser, because you're taking a very circuitous route. Did you consider it a contaminant, yes or no?

PERCY:

I can't answer a yes or no to that, unless I tell you what had happened is the fact that there was a lot of reports in the papers that farmers should not use a certain chemical continuously on a particular field because you could develop super-weeds that would ...

HUGHES:

Mr. Schmeiser, I'm trying to ask you questions so you can answer yes or no. Now, I asked you: "Did you consider this to be a contaminant and therefore did you phone a consultant?" And is your answer no?

PERCY:
No.

HUGHES:
Your *answer* is no?

PERCY:
Yes.

HUGHES:
Yes.

SCENE 8

PROJECTION (text):
Contamination

NADÈGE ADAM is interviewed by the PLAYWRIGHT at her Ottawa office.

NADÈGE:
"Contamination" is a new word because the act of, you know, pollen blowing from field to field has always happened in the past. But because now you have to create a distinction between GM crops and non-GM crops, you therefore have the term "contamination."

PLAYWRIGHT:
Nadège Adam, anti-GM food campaigner for the Council of Canadians.

NADÈGE:
See, people always thought that this was just a *Percy* story. But if you look at Canada right now, the better part of Western Canada is contaminated with Monsanto's seed.

PLAYWRIGHT:
The Council of Canadians: self-described as the country's largest citizens' organization, one that works to promote progressive social and economic policies in Canada.

JORDAN:
Known in some circles as a leftist lobby group run by the radical Maude Barlow.

MAUDE BARLOW happens to walk past NADÈGE's office at that moment.

NADÈGE:
Maude, this is the playwright I was telling you about.

29

BARLOW:
   Hello.

NADÈGE:
   Cuz what Monsanto would do is, like, they'd go out and take
   samples of plants on your land, do the testing, and then you'd
   get a letter telling you: "You either pay us fifteen dollars an acre
   or we're gonna take your behind to court." Right? And what was
   different with *Percy* is that he was, like, "Well, go ahead and take
   me to court, cuz I am not paying." Everybody else: "This is
   Monsanto." They're, like: "Okay, we'll pay." You know what I
   mean?

JORDAN:
   Ask her why Mr. Schmeiser didn't just call Monsanto when he
   first noticed that the canola didn't die.

NADÈGE:
   Because he was, like, "That's not my business, that's not my
   problem ... I'm not the one that put it there."

JORDAN:
   It was very clear that we had a patent on it.

NADÈGE:
   He's, like, "You're the one that contaminated my field. Why do I
   have to go and chase *you* down?!"

JORDAN:
   He *says* he had never heard of GM canola before it ... it just ...
   "flew onto his land."

NADÈGE:
   It never even entered into his mind: "Well, gee, I must make sure
   that this seed no longer grows on my field." He's, like, "I didn't
   put it there, oh well!"

JORDAN:
   When we commercialized this product back in '96, there was *all
   sorts* of advertising about it.

NADÈGE:

Oh! But if you're a farmer and you *see this*, you better make sure you call Monsanto.

JORDAN:

I mean, but Mr. Schmeiser apparently *lived in a vacuum* back then, even though he was the mayor of his town.

NADÈGE:

Because Monsanto, not only do they have these inspectors just, like, you know, parachuting onto your field any time of the day without you knowing, testing your fields. They also set up toll-free lines so, if your neighbour suspects you of growing Monsanto's canola, Monsanto's like:

NADÈGE'S COLLEAGUE:

"Call that phone line to tell on your neighbour!"

NADÈGE:

They will even give you a Monsanto leather jacket if you tell on your neighbour. It's the weirdest thing you have ever seen. It's unbelievable, but that's what they do.

JORDAN:

We warned him *before* he planted in 1998.

NADÈGE:

They know that this stuff is spreading! You know, it only takes, like, a very windy day and there you go: it's in your field, right?

JORDAN:

And when he didn't heed that warning, we had to take action.

NADÈGE:

And so that's what happened here. It's really Monsanto's game plan to go about contaminating as much land as possible so that GMO is a *fait accompli* that you can't fight anymore!

PLAYWRIGHT:

My conversation with Nadège made me wonder whether Percy knew about Monsanto's practices at the time that he found their seeds growing in his field. Nadège was suggesting that the introduction of Roundup Ready crops into farm communities across Canada was controversial and maybe even unwelcome in certain quarters ... even if most farmers were signing contracts and using it. Was it possible that Percy welcomed Monsanto's lawsuit as an opportunity to stand up for some farmers' rights?

SCENE 9

*At PERCY and LOUISE's house. The PLAYWRIGHT sneezes
and blows her nose.*

PERCY:
That's a nasty cold you've got there. (*yells*) LOUISE?!

LOUISE:
(*from another room in the house*) Yeah?!

PERCY:
When did you come down with it?

PLAYWRIGHT:
Oh ... a couple of days ago ... and I thought Montreal was cold.

PERCY:
You ain't seen nothing yet.

> *The PLAYWRIGHT laughs. LOUISE enters in a hurry.*

PERCY:
Louise, she needs ... Would you care for a hot drink? She's got a
cold, Louise.

PLAYWRIGHT:
That's okay ... I'm fine, thank you.

LOUISE:
Well, let me just get you some warm milk and honey or
something, dear. Percy it's cold in here; turn the heat up.

PERCY:
I could turn the heat up.

LOUISE:
Are you feeding yourself properly? You know you're eating for two now.

PLAYWRIGHT:
Thank you ... really, it's fine ...

LOUISE has already left to get the warm milk.

PLAYWRIGHT:
So, yeah ... um ... Percy, this is just something I wanted to follow up on from the other day about the beginning of your legal case. Um, I'm just wondering ... when you decided to go ahead and fight Monsanto's lawsuit ... uh ... was the community in Bruno supportive of you? They must have appreciated that you were at least standing up for their rights as farmers.

PERCY:
In ... in private I have a lot of support because people are so scared. When you have a Monsanto rep say to a farmer, "If you support Percy Schmeiser, we're going to come after you the same as we did him" ... When you have those threats made, and when they see how much we ... how much it's cost us to stand up to Monsanto ... Farmers would come and tell me how Monsanto would take them on fishing trips. They would take them to local restaurants here for a meal, and then they'd say negative things about me. So, that whole fear culture, you know, farmers will just capitulate ... they'll just give in when they find out it's cost me three hundred thousand dollars plus five years of our life.

LOUISE has returned with milk.

PLAYWRIGHT:
(*to LOUISE*) Thank you.

LOUISE:
You're welcome, dear.

LOUISE exits.

PERCY:
Now, where were we?

PLAYWRIGHT:
You were talking about the culture of fear ... but I would just ...
I'm just trying to understand something ... about when you first
discovered ... like ... as soon as you found out that Roundup
Ready canola was growing in your field, you felt that your rights
as a farmer were infringed?

PERCY:
Well, initially, um, back in 1997 and 1998 there was very little
information known about GMO canola, or contracts ... the rights
of farmers not being able to, um, grow their seed from year to
year. Because there was no information in our papers and the
government never said anything about GMOs. When I first
found out in 1998 that it was a patent on seeds, *you didn't know
what they were talking about.*

PLAYWRIGHT:
So, before you discovered it growing in your field, you didn't
know that Roundup Ready canola even existed?

PERCY:
That's right ... at that point ...

PLAYWRIGHT:
But weren't farmers in your area already growing the stuff?

PERCY:
You didn't know! See, what ... what happened, like, the local
seed dealer or chemical dealer – they'd get a call from a
company like Monsanto and they'd say, "Can you get us the
names of three or four farmers or whatever in the district here,
and invite them to a special meeting?"

*We see a group of farmers sit down to a Monsanto
informational meeting with some Monsanto propaganda
in front of them.*

And they called it a "Monsanto Informational Meeting." And you had a special invitation. And when you went there, you were wined and dined and you're told all the glories of this new thing that came up, you see?

Pause.

I was never invited.

PLAYWRIGHT:

This was the first time I had heard any details about how GM seeds were introduced into our food supply. The way Percy described it, it sounded really secretive. How could something as important as GMOs slip under the radar like that? Why were some farmers chosen and others excluded? Why didn't people outside the farming community have any idea that this was happening? Were companies like Monsanto hoping they could establish GM crops in Canada before the general public woke up to the issue?

SCENE 10

A Saskatoon courtroom.

HUGHES:
> My Lord, the plaintiffs now call Mr. Don Todd as the next witness.

> *Enter DON TODD. He swears in.*

PLAYWRIGHT:
> In the summer of 1998, Monsanto obtained a court order to take official samples of canola plants for testing from Percy Schmeiser's fields.

HUGHES:
> Mr. Todd, did you ever conduct an investigation in respect to samples of canola growing on Mr. Schmeiser's property?

TODD:
> Yes, I did. Under a court order, I went to the Schmeiser farm.

HUGHES:
> And do you recall what you did under the court order?

TODD:
> On the ... I believe it was the twelfth of August of 1998, I was instructed by my employer, Robinson Investigations, to proceed to the Percy Schmeiser farm in the Bruno district. On the following day, I picked up Mr. Jim Vancha in Saskatoon ...

> *JIM VANCHA enters.*

HUGHES:
> Mr. Vancha, can you identify yourself for the court, please?

VANCHA:

> James Vancha, associate manager of intellectual property,
> Monsanto Canada.

TODD:

> Mr. Vancha and I drove to the Bruno area in my half-ton truck.
> We found Mr. Schmeiser working in one of his fields. He came
> over to where we were waiting at the edge of the field.

> *ZAKRESKI examines PERCY, intercut with HUGHES*
> *examining TODD and VANCHA. CARLYLE MORITZ*
> *stands with PERCY to reflect the real scene in the field.*

ZAKRESKI:

> Mr. Schmeiser, do you remember August 13, 1998, meeting with
> a James Vancha or a Don Todd?

PERCY:

> Yes, I do.

HUGHES:

> Now, Mr. Todd, can you describe what happened?

TODD:

> I identified myself to Mr. Schmeiser, and Mr. Vancha did the
> same. Then I advised him that we were there under court order
> to collect samples from the parcels of land identified in the court
> order. And it was also my understanding that Mr. Schmeiser
> would accompany us while we did the inspection and sample
> taking ...

PERCY:

> And I said that I'm also supposed to receive a sample and I'll be
> going with you; and they said they have instructions that I'm to
> get a sample, but they have no instructions for me to go along.

> *Pause.*

TODD:

> I asked Mr. Schmeiser if he was going to accompany us on the
> sample taking. He declined to do so.

PERCY:

They were adamant I don't go with them.

HUGHES:

Why didn't Mr. Schmeiser want to go with you?

TODD's and VANCHA's contradictory replies overlap.

TODD:

He indicated that he had, I believe, some ailment, a sore leg or something.

VANCHA:

Mr. Schmeiser said he was busy swathing and didn't feel that he needed to come with us.

ZAKRESKI:

And what did you say, Mr. Schmeiser?

PERCY:

I said, "If I can't go with you, then you can't take a sample." And they said ...

TODD and VANCHA:

We got a court order and *we'll* take a sample!

PERCY:

And then they jumped into their vehicle, spun out of my field, and took off and drove north until they were out of my sight.

TODD and VANCHA exit.

PERCY:

And I never seen them anymore until about ... I would imagine somewheres around three o'clock. They drove back into the approach of the field.

TODD and VANCHA re-enter.

TODD:

And we presented to him his portion of the samples.

TODD hands over half of the sample bags to PERCY.

PERCY:
They had a bundle of plastic Ziploc bags, and they gave me those bags and asked me if they could take a picture of me receiving them.

VANCHA:
I took a picture of Mr. Todd giving Mr. Schmeiser those samples.

TODD and PERCY pose for the photo.

PERCY:
(*speaking to the PLAYWRIGHT in interview*) One of 'em even said that I had a sore leg! I'm a mountain climber, for Pete's sakes! I've never had a sore leg!

HUGHES:
Mr. Schmeiser ...

PLAYWRIGHT:
Percy has made two attempts to scale Mount Everest, has successfully climbed Mount Kilimanjaro, and has crossed the Sahara Desert.

PERCY:
They lied through their teeth! They said, "We got samples from your field, from all your fields." "Well," I said, "how could you take samples from all my fields?" I said, "I can see three fields from here." I said, "I never saw you in the field."

IIUGHES:
Mr. Schmeiser, the testimony that you've given differs from the testimony of Mr. Vancha and Mr. Todd!

PERCY returns to courtroom reality and answers reluctantly.

PERCY:
Yes.

HUGHES:

Notwithstanding that, it was your field and you could have gone wherever you liked, can we agree on that?

PERCY:

It was my field, but they left me in the field and drove off.

HUGHES:

Yes, but for a fellow that climbed Mounts Kilimanjaro and Everest and crossed the Sahara, a short walk back to your truck wouldn't have been an insurmountable obstacle, would it?

PERCY:

No.

HUGHES:

Okay. So, you could have gotten in your truck and done one of two things: you could have followed them or you could have gone about and sampled some of them all on your own, couldn't you?

PERCY:

I could have followed them if I knew where they went, but I had to walk about a mile to get my truck.

HUGHES:

Or you could have said, "To heck with them, I'm going to take my own samples."

PERCY:

Hindsight is a great thing.

HUGHES:

And you could have said, "If you won't let me accompany you, get off my land."

PERCY:

I exactly did say that, and they said they got a court ...

HUGHES:

So, you had those two choices. Now, did you phone your lawyer and say there's something wrong with the sample taking and I'm not very happy about it?

PERCY:

I didn't contact my lawyer that day, but I did ...

HUGHES:

Did you instruct your lawyer to write ...

ZAKRESKI:

Objection ...

HUGHES:

... either to the court or anybody else?

ZAKRESKI:

I object ...

HUGHES:

Well, it seems that this witness is trying to *make* something of the conflicting testimony between him and Mr. Todd and Mr. Vancha. So, let me ask this question: there was no letter sent by your lawyer to the lawyers for Monsanto complaining about the nature of the sample taking?

PERCY:

I would not be aware of that.

HUGHES:

Not aware of any formal complaint about the sample taking. Thank you.

HUGHES bulldozes on with evidence about the samples.

Now, Your Lordship will hear evidence that these samples collected by Don Todd and James Vancha, when they were tested, proved that well over 90 percent in fact contained the Roundup Ready gene.

ZAKRESKI:
My Lord, I would like to make a point here ...

HUGHES:
That is consistent with a *commercial* grade of seed ...

ZAKRESKI:
There were more tests done than what Mr. Hughes has spoken about ...

HUGHES:
Now, these samples were tested to detect the presence of the gene in several different ways ...

ZAKRESKI:
There were *independent* tests done on these samples which show a far lower rate of conta—

HUGHES:
Including with a very, very sophisticated process called an electrophoresis test conducted at Monsanto headquarters in St. Louis.

ZAKRESKI:
And in fact, the sampling and testing is, I would call it, a mess of different results, different people ...

HUGHES:
And in all the tests of the defendant's canola, the results were more or less the same ...

ZAKRESKI:
With the major problem being that the Monsanto tests were carried out internally by Monsanto employees!

HUGHES:
And the samples were, on all occasions, found to be over 95 percent resistant to Roundup!

Sound of gavel.

SCENE 11

An upscale restaurant in Ottawa. TONY CREBER in
interview with the PLAYWRIGHT.

PLAYWRIGHT:

So, this is 95 percent resistance on the 1998 samples ... agh ...
why does everything have to be ninety-something!

CREBER:

So, okay, let's start with the dates. We have Year 1 and Year 2.
Year 1 is 1997, when Mr. Schmeiser says he found it growing in
his field and he does his test. Sixty percent of his test spray area
is resistant to Roundup. Now, Roundup Ready canola was only
introduced in 1996 ... So, how did so much of it get into his fields
in the first place in 1997?

PLAYWRIGHT:

Well, Percy gave several explanations during the trial. He says
cross-pollination, seed falling off trucks as they passed his
field ... In 1996, there was a huge windstorm that apparently
blew swaths of canola plants onto his fields from a neighbo—
You're not buying any of that, are you?

CREBER:

Okay ... okay, I understand; the seed got onto his field somehow
"without him knowing." To end up with 60 percent in three acres
by it just ... *blowing in* is a pretty high percentage. But *fine*, let's
assume for the sake of argument that it did blow in. But then he
sprayed Roundup on it and planted his 1998 crop with *those seeds*.

PLAYWRIGHT:

Yes, but so what? Percy *owns* his property, doesn't he? So, doesn't
that mean he owns whatever ends up growing there? He can do
whatever the hell he wants with it!

CREBER:
No. Not if it has a patent on it. Patent infringement is a type of *trespass*. He *trespassed*.

PLAYWRIGHT:
But he didn't know there was a patent on it at the time!

CREBER:
Well, unfortunately ... or fortunately ... we will never know exactly what Mr. Schmeiser knew, but that still doesn't refute the science of the case. Because even if that original seed in 1997 came in by *natural* means, it still could not produce progeny that, when planted in 1998, created a crop that is 95 percent resistant to Roundup!

PLAYWRIGHT:
(*to audience*) But was that true? I had no idea what science Creber was referring to. Why was that number so damning? At this point, I was getting *completely confused* about the thrust of Monsanto's patent infringement suit. Were they trying to prove that the GM seed couldn't have possibly arrived on his land in 1997 through natural means? Or were they trying to show that, even if it did, he knowingly did something afterward to enhance it into a Roundup Ready crop?

SCENE 12

A Saskatoon courtroom.

HUGHES:
I call, as the next witness for the plaintiff, Dr. Keith Downey.
Dr. Downey.

DR. KEITH DOWNEY enters.

PLAYWRIGHT:
Dr. Keith Downey is a Canadian agricultural scientist who, in the
early 1970s, engineered the transformation of oilseed rape into
Canada's *number-one* agricultural product: canola. Today, canola
is used for deep-frying McDonald's french fries. It is also the
primary vegetable oil in Hellmann's mayonnaise. Canola
contributes $15.4 billion annually to Canada's economy.

HUGHES:
I would like to have this witness qualified to speak as an expert
in the area of canola.

ZAKRESKI:
(*sighs*) I have no objection to this witness's qualifications.

HUGHES:
Thank you. Now, Dr. Downey, did you prepare a report for use in
these proceedings and do you have a copy in front of you?

DOWNEY:
I did and there is.

A COURT CLERK brings in a voluminous report for DOWNEY.

HUGHES:
And in your report you were asked to address several matters.
Can we start with matter number one?

DOWNEY:

Yes. Matter number one: "What is the effect of wind, spillage, insect, and other such phenomena in crop migration from a field, roadway, or elsewhere, to another field?

HUGHES:

And your *brief* answer?

DOWNEY:

My answer is: these phenomena do have an effect in crop migration but not to such a degree as would account for the amount of Roundup-tolerant canola found growing on Mr. Schmeiser's fields in 1997.

PLAYWRIGHT:

1997, Year 1.

HUGHES:

And can you tell us, in a nutshell, how you conclude that?

DOWNEY:

I'll try.

He turns to audience skeptically.

All plants and animals have two sets of chromosomes, one contributed by the mother and the other ...

DOWNEY keeps testifying while the PLAYWRIGHT clarifies for the audience ...

PLAYWRIGHT:

In a nutshell, Keith Downey explained that he had collected canola pod samples from the public rights-of-way around Percy's fields in 1997. Dr. Downey then grew out the *progeny* from those pods into fully grown plants. He then sprayed those plants with Roundup to see which ones were tolerant and which ones were killed. According to the laws of inheritance, if a sample plant he took was the result of crop migration, only one in four of its seeds should be killed by Roundup.

DOWNEY:
(*winding up his explanation*) ... but in this case all the plants we grew out survived.

HUGHES:
And perhaps you can give us the *conclusion* of that background scientific information?

DOWNEY:
Well, it's very strong evidence that the plants found growing in Mr. Schmeiser's fields in 1997 were from a Roundup-tolerant variety and not the result of outcrossing.

HUGHES:
In other words, he deliberately planted it.

DOWNEY:
Well, I don't *know* if he planted it, but ...

    Sound of judge's gavel.

JORDAN:
(*reading from a newspaper article*) "The world's most prominent canola scientist has testified that Percy Schmeiser's story doesn't make sense!" See: this isn't just me speaking; look at how the media reported it: (*continues reading*) "Keith Downey explained in court today that if Mr. Schmeiser's canola had been the result of cross-pollination, then the chance that Monsanto investigators managed to pick six plants that all had Roundup-tolerant seeds was only one in ten and ..." a hell of a lot of zeros.

HUGHES:
Can you actually give that number in an expression, Dr. Downey?

DOWNEY:
Oh boy!

HUGHES:
Is it billions and billions, or something like that?

DOWNEY:

Well, it's one with nineteen zeros after it, whatever that comes out to, and I consider such odds to be highly improbable.

LAB TECHNICIAN 5:

Said Dr. Downey, known in some circles as the "Father of Canola"!

SCENE 13

CLARK:

(*sighs*) It's not true! If it really *was* 95 percent resistant, I would not believe Schmeiser; it is not possible to happen that way *biologically*.

PLAYWRIGHT:

I consulted Dr. Ann Clark at the University of Guelph about the legitimacy of Monsanto's scientific evidence at the trial.

CLARK:

But their numbers were contested. Monsanto *said* that the samples that Todd and Vancha collected were "95 to 98 percent contamination." But that is a standard dogmatic number.

PLAYWRIGHT:

What do you mean?

CLARK:

It's a number Monsanto uses on *every* farmer each time they threaten with a lawsuit. The evidence is always "it was 95 percent resistant, it was 95 percent resistant." But then when Schmeiser didn't cave, *then* they had to drag the samples out of the freezer and analyze them up, because until then they hadn't been forced to do it. One batch of samples went to Monsanto for testing; the other went to Schmeiser's analysts at the University of Manitoba: Lyle Friesen and Rene Van Acker.

SCENE 14

*DR. RENE VAN ACKER and LYLE FRIESEN in interview
with the PLAYWRIGHT, at a bar in Winnipeg.*

FRIESEN:
Monsanto testified that the samples they collected were all
95 percent resistant. Well ... they sure weren't testing the same
stuff that we tested.

VAN ACKER:
Yeah. Our results definitely conflicted with theirs.

They laugh.

PLAYWRIGHT:
Lyle Friesen and Rene Van Acker, two weed scientists at the
University of Manitoba.

VAN ACKER:
But, I mean, the case itself wasn't ... I mean, personally ... Lyle
can comment on it, but the case wasn't very well prepared from
a biological perspective ...

FRIESEN laughs.

PLAYWRIGHT:
What do you mean?

VAN ACKER:
I mean, there was a lot of baloney and incomplete facts.

PLAYWRIGHT:
Can you give me an example?

FRIESEN:
Like Monsanto, for instance, with their ... with the collection of
their samples ... I mean, when you're gonna go get *evidence* of

what's growing in the field? I mean, they went out and collected pod samples about mid-August and what did they do with those pods? They went and stuck them in plastic Ziploc bags!

FRIESEN and VAN ACKER laugh loudly.

PLAYWRIGHT:
Oh, you're not supposed to do that?

FRIESEN:
No! About half or three-quarters of them moulded! So, we couldn't even grow them out *to* test them. The ones that we could grow out were only testing between ... well, some were trace, some were 40 to 65 percent resistant.

VAN ACKER:
And then you have Keith Downey and other Monsanto people commenting on how, you know, canola's not an active volunteer and all that.

PLAYWRIGHT:
Active ... what?

VAN ACKER:
Volunteer ... they were saying canola doesn't spread easily.

FRIESEN:
Yeah.

VAN ACKER:
I mean, at that point those guys ... they're, like, *way* out of their depth in terms of, you know, talking out the top of their hat ... they didn't know what they were talkin' about!

FRIESEN:
Canola is an *extremely* effective volunteer.

VAN ACKER:
A quarter of all fields in Manitoba have volunteer canola infestations. To suggest that GM seeds couldn't spread ... I mean, no problems *at all*, you know?

FRIESEN:
Confinement is next to impossible.

VAN ACKER:
Oh yeah. Confinement is a Pandora's box!

PLAYWRIGHT:
Did you manage to get this message across when you testified at the trial?

Pause.

VAN ACKER:
Well ... not really.

FRIESEN:
Nope.

PLAYWRIGHT:
Why not?

VAN ACKER:
Because at the time, we just didn't understand the nature of the case.

FRIESEN:
Nope.

VAN ACKER:
You have to remember ... this was kinda like the first case of its kind in Canada.

FRIESEN:
A precedent.

VAN ACKER:
Everyone was making things up as they went along. I mean, we never even *met* with Zakreski to discuss the case before we testified.

FRIESEN:
Nope.

PLAYWRIGHT:
Well, why did Zakreski choose you guys to testify?

Pause.

VAN ACKER:
Who knows? I think it was basically an accident that we testified.

PERCY:
It was no accident!

PLAYWRIGHT in interview with ZAKRESKI.

ZAKRESKI:
It's true. Before I called in Lyle and Rene, I had two scientists
lined up to witness from Ag' Canada. They were going to back up
Percy's theory about how Monsanto's seed got into his crop. They
even wrote a report, which I sent to Monsanto with my notice of
expert witness. But then a few weeks before the trial started, I got
summoned to Ag' Canada's offices at the University of
Saskatchewan. I was, like, grilled by the program director about
"what involvement" was intended for their scientists at the trial.
I tried to explain to everyone that I just wanted a qualified,
honest opinion without it being binding on Ag' Canada. A week
later, I receive a letter from my Ag' Canada witnesses stating that
they now agreed with Dr. Downey's rebuttal of their report! So, I
couldn't use them as witnesses anymore.

PLAYWRIGHT:
I looked into the plausibility of government regulatory agencies
being pressured by Monsanto. I found dozens of articles on the
Internet about Health Canada scientists who had attempted to
block the approval of bovine growth hormone, a genetically
modified hormone created by ...

CLARK:
Monsanto.

PLAYWRIGHT:
Monsanto ... to increase milk production in cows. One of these scientists, Dr. Margaret Haydon, testified before a senate committee in 1998 that she was removed from a study about the safety of bovine growth hormone when she refused to approve it. Dr. Haydon also testified that her notes and files from the study were stolen from a locked cabinet in her office.

CLARK:
It says here that she was privy to bribe offers being made by Monsanto to some of her senior colleagues at Health Canada.

PLAYWRIGHT:
Dr. Haydon and two other scientists were fired by Health Canada for insubordination.

SCENE 15

JORDAN:

No, no, no, no, no. Look: in the end, our numbers were *not* contested at the trial.

PLAYWRIGHT:

But Lyle Friesen's results were very different from Monsanto's ...

JORDAN:

Well, right. So ... right ... *Lyle Friesen.* (*laughs*) Lyle Friesen says he tested Percy's twenty-seven bags at "0 to 67 percent" – the seed from the twenty-seven bags that Percy stored in his basement. And I'm not suggesting that anything was done to them, but ... Right? Right? Who knows? We don't know. We just go by what Percy *said.* But what we *do* know – and this to me is the clincher – there's a sample that comes to us for testing from Humboldt Flour Mill.

A bag of seed falls from the sky, landing next to JORDAN with a loud thump.

The Humboldt Flour Mill: where Percy had his 1998 seed treated after harvest.

MORRIS HOFMANN enters.

This was a sample that Monsanto *never* touched and Percy *never* touched; it went straight from the Humboldt Flour Mill to Lyle Friesen. And when Lyle Friesen tested *that* sample, it was 95 to 98 percent resistant – the same as our numbers.

Scene shifts to a Saskatoon courtroom.

ZAKRESKI:

Mr. Hofmann, do you recall having any discussions with Mr. Schmeiser after it was discovered that you had sent these samples to Monsanto?

PROJECTION (text):
Morris Hofmann, assistant manager of farm supplies,
Humboldt Flour Mill

HOFMANN:
He phoned me one Saturday morning.

ZAKRESKI:
And in that conversation, did he ask you ...

PERCY:
How am I to know that those samples are from my crop?

ZAKRESKI:
Did he ask you that?

HOFMANN:
I don't understand the question.

ZAKRESKI:
How was Mr. Schmeiser to know that those samples were from
his crop? Did he ask you that?

HOFMANN:
No.

ZAKRESKI:
Do you recall him telling you that he doesn't have any way to
know that the samples are from his crop?

HOFMANN:
I don't think that ever came up in the conversation. No.

*This court sequence remains suspended for a moment
while PERCY speaks in interview.*

PERCY:
(*to PLAYWRIGHT*) The seed I took in 1998 to Humboldt Flour
Mill to be treated had chaff in it. It was not cleaned. What Morris
Hofmann submitted to Lyle Friesen was perfectly clean. And
what did Morris Hofmann confess to me afterward? He was a

Monsanto agent for Humboldt Flour Mill. He said he took Monsanto seed, said they were mine, and sent them to Winnipeg to be tested. He came to *me*.

PERCY approaches HOFMANN.

I met him in Humboldt, and he said ...

HOFMANN is about to speak, but PERCY speaks for him.

PERCY:

He *admitted* he was taken on trips by Monsanto. Weekends. He was wined and dined by Monsanto. He told me afterward where he got the seed. He came to me and, um, I'll tell you what he said. If you turn off your tape recorder, I'll tell you about it, if you just turn it off for a second.

Pause.

PLAYWRIGHT:

I made a gesture, pretending to stop my digital recorder, but I didn't turn it off. I just wanted to have a record of what Percy was about to say for myself – I knew I could never use the testimony onstage. Percy told me that Hofmann decided to make a confession at that time because he had just been diagnosed with a terminal illness. He described to me, in minute detail, Hofmann's final act of contrition.

Pause.

I couldn't corroborate Percy's story, though, because Hofmann did indeed die in 2002.

SCENE 16

A Saskatoon courtroom.

HUGHES:
Now, Mr. Schmeiser, you were present in court throughout this trial, correct?

PERCY:
Here?

HUGHES:
Yes. Here.

PERCY:
Yes.

HUGHES:
You heard the evidence of every witness?

PERCY:
Yes.

HUGHES:
And you gave evidence yourself, of course?

PERCY:
Yes.

HUGHES:
As you're doing now. There's conflict between your testimony and the testimony of a number of witnesses; can we agree on that?

PERCY:
On a number of witnesses, yes, it could even be more than that.

HUGHES:

Thank you. There's conflict between your testimony and what went on at the meeting between you and Mr. Vancha and Mr. Todd in your fields in August of 1998. Are you calling Mr. Todd and Mr. Vancha liars?

PERCY:

Those are your words.

HUGHES:

No, I'm asking you. Are you calling them liars?

PERCY:

I don't think I would ever really call anybody a liar.

HUGHES:

What are you calling them, then?

PERCY:

You know, I really don't know how to answer that.

HUGHES:

There's conflict with respect to the testing of samples taken from your fields, correct?

PERCY:

Yes.

HUGHES:

Are you saying that somebody from Monsanto tampered with the samples?

PERCY:

Those are your words.

HUGHES:

There's conflict between your testimony and the meeting you had with Mr. Hofmann?

PERCY:
Very much so.

HUGHES:
Are you calling Mr. Hofmann a liar?

PERCY:
Again those are your words.

HUGHES:
Is it your position that all these people have conspired against you by telling lies, by tampering with samples, and otherwise trying to defeat the process of this court simply in order to humiliate and embarrass you?

Pause.

PERCY:
Sorry, could you repeat the question?

HUGHES:
Is it your position that all these people, and possibly more, have told lies, have tampered with samples, and have otherwise dealt with the evidence in order to humiliate and embarrass you?

PERCY:
I would answer that it's their opinions, and my opinion was different.

HUGHES:
Thank you, those are my questions.

SCENE 17

PROJECTION (text):
Resistance

PLAYWRIGHT:
The dictionary definition of the verb "to resist" is "to stop the course of," "to successfully oppose," or "to prevent from penetrating." And yet, as we know from the practice of inoculation, true resistance is born through exposure to small doses of infection. Although Percy had to tolerate Monsanto's presence in his fields and them digging into his private life, his resistance to the company seemed to be getting stronger the longer that he exposed himself to their legal assault.

Watson and Crick, on the other hand, met with little resistance when they announced their central dogma to the world. Their DNA theory was instantly welcomed by a 1950s Western society giddy with industrial success. They compared activity inside the living cell to production on an assembly line. DNA is like the CEO of a factory and holds the plans for an invention called life. Those plans are read by manager proteins, translated into action items for worker proteins, and finally followed like a manual to build an organism's inherited traits: a yellow blossom on a cash crop, or a crop of blond hair on a Monsanto executive.

Watson and Crick's theory transformed biology into a popular and futuristic enterprise. If DNA exercised absolute control over inherited traits in living organisms, living organisms could now be *modified* simply by tinkering with their DNA. This sensational corollary of the Watson-Crick theory spawned a multi-billion-dollar industry overnight. Resistance was futile.

ALTOSAAR:
See, there's a difference between science and fear. Fear is an *emotion*; science is *a process*.

PLAYWRIGHT:
Dr. Illimar Altosaar: professor of biochemistry, microbiology, and immunology, University of Ottawa.

ALTOSAAR:
Now, in this case, someone alleges a crime was committed. *None of us* were at the scene. We don't know what happened. *Supposition.* And I'm trying to divine or induce ... by induction – this is what scientists do – what were the farmer's motives, based on what he actually *did*?

PLAYWRIGHT:
What did he actually do?

ALTOSAAR:
Well, Monsanto went to visit Mr. Schmeiser and said, "Listen! In Canada the law says that this winning aspect of this gene saying that you can spray all the plutonium, tutonium, nuclear chemicals on me, I'll still grow as a beautiful yellow flower in the springtime. *Resistance*! Resistance! That's *ours* – no matter what you may believe or think about how it got here!"
And the farmer has just, apparently just, with his actions or whatever said, "I don't give a damn! I know who you are. And the Naomi Cheims or Heims ... or whoever she is ... that branding person in Toronto ..."

PLAYWRIGHT:
(*overlapping*) Naomi *Klein* is the award-winning author of *No Logo* and *The Shock Doctrine*.

ALTOSAAR:
"... they're all on my side, they're all going to be on my side in this argument, so why should I care?"

PLAYWRIGHT:
(*to ALTOSAAR*) I understand that your microbiology research has been funded, in part, by grants from a lot of corporations, including Monsanto.

ALTOSAAR:

And? So?! Why do you despise corporations? Is it because the sort of soft, *left-wing* socialists in your federal government have gone along with the United Nations and developing countries of the world, you know, on the "hate corporate America bandwagon"? If Petro-Canada is a venture as much as your theatre company is a venture, it's a good business; why would we ... why would we attack you?

What?! You close people up in a filthy old building? Stuffy air for *two hours*? And then you walk on the dusty floor and the dust comes up and asbestos in their lungs! How can you do that? That's *unhealthy*; I can bring you a thousand articles to say that's *bad* what you do. "Let's attack her."

And then, you know, *Maclean's* and *Saturday Night* and the *New Yorker* and *Harper's* just come and *bury* you. You're dead. And you say, "On what grounds?" Like, "Why? It's just theatre."

SCENE 18

HUGHES:

My Lord, may I have a moment just to see if my next witness is out there?

HUGHES chats with his surprise witness in an antechamber before calling him into the courtroom. HUGHES returns with WESLEY NIEBRUGGE.

It will be Mr. Wesley Niebrugge.

CARLYLE MORITZ enters.

ZAKRESKI:

My Lord, you are not entitled to call a witness to contradict another witness on a matter that's collateral, or things could be endless.

HUGHES:

This is not a collateral issue.

ZAKRESKI:

They are putting a witness on the stand to say, "Mr. Schmeiser's farmhand, Carlyle Moritz, said something to me," which frankly is of no use at all. It's hearsay; it's not proof of the facts.

HUGHES:

Carlyle Moritz was the man who did some of the swathing, he did some of the spraying. He is the hired hand of the man, his *agent*, if you like.

Pause as HUGHES waits for the judge's ruling.

Thank you, My Lord.

WESLEY NIEBRUGGE swears in.

HUGHES:

Mr. Niebrugge, you're a farmer in the Bruno area?

NIEBRUGGE:
That's correct.

HUGHES:
And you also work at the Imperial Oil?

NIEBRUGGE:
Yeah.

HUGHES:
Do you know Carlyle Moritz?

NIEBRUGGE:
Yes, I do.

HUGHES:
And what do you know of him?

NIEBRUGGE:
Well, he works for Mr. Schmeiser.

HUGHES:
Did you have occasion to discuss with him, in the fall and winter of '97, Mr. Schmeiser's farming practices?

NIEBRUGGE:
Yes.

HUGHES:
Can you relate to the court what those discussions were?

NIEBRUGGE:
Well, it was more or less that he had said that they were seeding the Roundup Ready canola.

HUGHES:
Anything else?

NIEBRUGGE:
And that they had sprayed it with Roundup.

HUGHES:
Okay. No further questions.

ZAKRESKI cross-examines NIEBRUGGE.

ZAKRESKI:
Mr. Niebrugge, do you do any business for Monsanto?

NIEBRUGGE:
We do sell some of their products, yes.

ZAKRESKI:
Do you sell Roundup?

NIEBRUGGE:
Yes, we do.

ZAKRESKI:
Do you wear any Monsanto clothing?

NIEBRUGGE:
I have a Monsanto jacket.

ZAKRESKI:
Is it a leather jacket?

NIEBRUGGE:
No.

ZAKRESKI:
Were you offered anything for the information you've given?

NIEBRUGGE:
No.

ZAKRESKI:
Did you attend the Brier this year, sir?

INTERJECTING VOICE:
The Brier is Canada's annual national curling tournament.

NIEBRUGGE:
  Yes, I did attend.

ZAKRESKI:
  Who paid for that?   ·

NIEBRUGGE:
  Well, it was Monsanto ...

ZAKRESKI:
  Did you sit in Monsanto's box seat?

NIEBRUGGE:
  Yes.

ZAKRESKI:
  Did you drink their liquor?

NIEBRUGGE:
  Yes.

ZAKRESKI:
  Lots of it? It was free, right?

NIEBRUGGE:
  Yeah.

ZAKRESKI:
  And when was Carlyle supposed to have made this statement to
  you?

NIEBRUGGE:
  Oh, I don't really remember the exact date. Somewhere between
  the fall of 1997 and the spring of 1999, before they came out to
  talk to me.

ZAKRESKI:
  Sometime during an eighteen-month period "before Monsanto
  came out to talk to you"?

      Pause.

NIEBRUGGE:
Yeah.

ZAKRESKI:
I have no further questions.

SCENE 19

The PLAYWRIGHT in interview with PERCY at his home.

PERCY:
The trial ended on the twenty-second of June. Judge MacKay
said he would render his judgment by the first week in August ...
Well, the first week in August came ... we heard nothing.
September, October, November ... nothing. Shortly before
Christmas, we get a notice from the federal court. The judge said
he would render his judgment by the first of February. The first
of February comes ... no judgment. Another week goes by,
another week, another week ... I think it was five times he
postponed it. I got a call from a CBC reporter during that time,
calling me for updates. She says to me, "Well, Percy, who do you
think your judge is golfing with today?"

The sound of a ball being putted and falling into a hole.

PLAYWRIGHT:
March 29, 2001. Federal trial judge Andrew MacKay finds Percy
Schmeiser guilty of patent infringement.

Sound of gavel. Blackout.

END ACT ONE

ACT TWO

SCENE 1

PROJECTION (text):
Life, Part 2

PLAYWRIGHT:
(*to audience*) I've become interested in the parallels between the work I do making documentary theatre and the work that biotech companies do making genetically modified seeds.

To begin with, we are both in the business of ... life. We use life as raw material and we modify it in order to produce something that we then call our "invention."

We both describe our mission as "making the world a better place" – Monsanto by feeding a hungry and growing world; me by telling stories in which a multiplicity of voices reflects something I perceive to be important about the world.
But we are also both susceptible along the way to ... outside influence.

The PLAYWRIGHT is having an ultrasound done.

ULTRASOUND TECHNICIAN:
So, you really want to know?

PLAYWRIGHT:
Yup.

ULTRASOUND TECHNICIAN:
(*after examining her*) Well, it looks like you got yourself another little girl in there.

ULTRASOUND TECHNICIAN exits.

The PLAYWRIGHT in interview with PERCY. LOUISE
brings in soup.

LOUISE:
Now, this should do the trick.

PERCY:
Oooh ... Louise's corn chowder: that'll fix you right up.

LOUISE:
Careful. It may be a little hot still.

PLAYWRIGHT:
That's perfect. Thank you.

LOUISE:
I make it for my grandkids when they've got a cold.

PERCY:
I can't remember when I had *my* last cold. Probably years ago.
(*chuckles*)

LOUISE:
There's more where that came from; just holler.

LOUISE exits. A moment of silence while the PLAYWRIGHT
sips soup.

PLAYWRIGHT:
Percy, I want to thank you so much for all the time you've spent
with me over the past two weeks. I can't believe I'm already
going back home tomorrow.

PERCY:
Well, time flies when you're so busy, eh?

PLAYWRIGHT:
Yeah ... exactly. So ... I just have a few last questions today that
are a bit more philosophical in nature ...

PERCY:

Well, I'm not much of a philosopher ...

PLAYWRIGHT:

You can just say whatever comes to mind, instinctively ...

PERCY:

All right, just ask me!

PLAYWRIGHT:

Okay ... okay ... Um, what do you like best about farming?

PERCY:

Well, uh, I really loved farming all my life. I could always find a
sort of relaxation. It gave me time to think about things when I
would come out here on a tractor and be away. Sometimes I
would do a night shift; I'd work all night just to watch the stars
and stuff. Your closeness, um, to nature ... Like, we have a lot of
geese here ... ducks ... and our, our ... and foxes and coyotes and
a lot of times these animals like a fox or a coyote would follow
along your equipment all day long while you worked ... just stay
right with you all day. And then during the year, you see that
new life, the growth of life, planting seeds, seeing how the plants
come up, how that grows, you know, into, into, um ... A matter
of three months or a hundred days, how a seed grows into a
plant that produces seeds and another life. That's what you see
every day here. So, so when you see that or you see, you know ...

   Pause.

I think that once you have that, um, it always remains with you.

SCENE 2

*PERCY at a press conference speaking about Judge
MacKay's ruling.*

PERCY:

I have lost fifty years of work because of a company's genetically
altered seed getting into my canola ...

PROJECTION (text):
Percy's statement to the press, March 2001

PERCY:

... destroying what I've worked for, destroying my property, and
getting sued on top of it.

JORDAN:

Monsanto feels this decision is good news for *Canadians*, all of
whom will benefit from the innovative work that is going on
across this country to produce more abundant and nutritious food.

PROJECTION (text):
Monsanto press release, March 2001

PERCY:

It will take totally all of my wife's and my retirement funds that
we've worked for all our lives to pay the legal bills for this case.

JORDAN:

Perhaps most important, the more than thirty thousand
Canadian farmers who have signed agreements with Monsanto
can now rest assured their commitment to fair play is secure.
This ruling levels the playing field for *everyone*.

The PLAYWRIGHT in interview with NADÈGE.

NADÈGE:

Around the same time that, uh, Percy got his first, you know,
verdict against him in the lower court, we, the Council of

Canadians, sort of made a statement, um, to the press in support of Percy, and I shouldn't say it was a *huge* backlash, but I never had ... I have never had members *call*, call in here and complain about whatever action the Council of Canadians takes on.

You see, Monsanto's smear campaign during the trial was so effective because what they did is, Monsanto kept alleging in the press that Percy *stole* their seeds. But they never substantiated those allegations *in court*. They managed to convince the judge somehow that he infringed their patent, but they never could prove that he obtained the seeds illegally – which is a fact that never really got reported in the press. So, the accusation just stuck in people's minds.

PLAYWRIGHT:
And I guess you have to respond to your membership's opinions.

NADÈGE:
Well, yeah. We're a member-based organization; we have no choice. Plus we have to consider the larger cause – the anti-GM cause. The whole idea of tying up the issue to one individual was very risky. So, I am ashamed to say that at first that's one of the reasons why we sort of, you know, we were in support of, but sort of kept our distance from, his case.

The PLAYWRIGHT in interview with SISTER CATHERINE FAIRBAIRN.

SISTER CATHERINE:
When he lost the case, I was watching on TV from Ottawa when he came out of the courtroom. I thought he was going to *bawl*! I felt so sorry for him. He was *all alone* in the TV shot, coming out of the court, like, his lawyer wasn't even there! It was, like, *nobody was with him*!

PLAYWRIGHT:
Sister Catherine Fairbairn.

SISTER CATHERINE:
He had sent his wife, Louise, down to California with one of their daughters because she had apparently found the whole thing,

like, very difficult. And he said, after the judgment, he walked in the door to his house ... and there was nobody at home waiting for him.

Sound of PERCY's home phone ringing.

But then the phone rang.

PERCY lets it ring a few times before answering.

SISTER CATHERINE:
And he answered.

PERCY picks up the phone.

PERCY:
Hello?

SISTER CATHERINE:
And it was me!

PLAYWRIGHT:
Sister Catherine Fairbairn is a member of the Ottawa chapter of the Grey Sisters of the Immaculate Conception.

SISTER CATHERINE:
It was *me* calling!

PERCY:
Yes?

SISTER CATHERINE:
It was me! And I said, "Percy, this is not the end, this is just the beginning." And he said ...

PERCY:
I'll never forget this.

SISTER CATHERINE;
And he said, "I'll never forget this."

SCENE 3

SISTER CATHERINE:
The Grey Sisters were one of the first ones to get involved and ...
and really sort of support Percy as any sort of a group.

PLAYWRIGHT:
What got you so interested in him in the first place?

SISTER CATHERINE:
Well, I hardly know how I first got interested. I read lots, and in
some paper I saw an article about this Percy Schmeiser, and I
started, like, to do some research and I ... I learned ... "My
goodness, they're senior citizens!" And then I ... And so I just did
a paper on them.

PLAYWRIGHT:
Excerpt from *Social Justice Network*, Sister Catherine's newsletter.

SISTER CATHERINE:
"A Modern-Day Story of David and Goliath." Percy is seventy
years of age and lives on his small farm with his wife, Louise.

PLAYWRIGHT:
Um ... Percy's farm is not small ... it's more than a thousand acres.

SISTER CATHERINE:
After I first read about their conflict with Monsanto, I called
Percy and sent him a "widow's mite" donation. When we spoke, I
knew that I was talking to a man of truth and courage, a man
who refuses to buckle under the harassment and accusations of
a large multinational corporation, a modern-day David armed
with faith and truth venturing forth to take on a seemingly
impossible battle with a Goliath!

*Other actors applaud to suggest strong reactions from
SISTER CATHERINE's readers.*

SISTER CATHERINE:
Well, I never got such a reaction to any former paper as I did when I wrote about Percy. So, then ... then I decided we have to get some more coverage for Percy because the media is the answer here. If you want to get people to know what really happened here, like, big media has to talk about it. So, after he lost that first case, I decided to write to the *Toronto Star*.

SISTER CATHERINE's letter to JOHN HONDERICH.

To Mr. John Honderich, publisher, the *Toronto Star*.

JOHN HONDERICH enters.

Dear Mr. Honderich, I have been crusading to help one small farmer and his wife in their quest for justice ...

HONDERICH:
Dear Sister Catherine, I want to thank you for the story tip. I have passed it on to Mary-Deanne Shears in editorial for consideration.

MARY-DEANNE SHEARS appears and takes the letter from HONDERICH.

I think there is a good story here. Sincerely yours, John A. Honderich, publisher, the *Toronto Star*.

SISTER CATHERINE celebrates.

SISTER CATHERINE:
The *Toronto Star*!

SHEARS:
One of the wonders of nature is its ability to propagate itself.

PLAYWRIGHT:
Toronto Star editorial.

SHEARS:
A single seed, caught on a gust of wind or hitching a ride on bird or beast can carry a plant's progeny far afield.

SISTER CATHERINE:
Dear Mary-Deanne Shears,

SHEARS:
But a disappointing decision by a federal court judge threatened to turn these wonders against farmers. This is a dangerous ruling.

SISTER CATHERINE:
Thank you for your excellent editorial! I am an ardent fan of the *Toronto Star*.

SHEARS:
Schmeiser did not want genetically modified crops in his field. He was just stuck with them when they showed up on their own.

SISTER CATHERINE:
I love the editorial page with its *real* analysis of issues and your superb writers who go to the heart of the matter.

SHEARS:
No one can control the flow of genes through nature. That's what makes it so wonderful, and so dangerous to tamper with.

SISTER CATHERINE:
God bless you. This makes my day special.

SHEARS:
We hope Schmeiser appeals this decision and can find the financial help he needs to continue his suit against Monsanto.

SISTER CATHERINE:
Gratefully, Sister Catherine Fairbairn, Grey Sisters of the Immaculate Conception.

> *SISTER CATHERINE starts a new letter:*

Dear Peter Mansbridge!

SCENE 4

An auditorium in Delhi, India. DR. VANDANA SHIVA stands at a podium, speaking with a booming voice into a microphone.

SHIVA:

(*thick Indian-British accent*) GM foods are not equivalent to non-GM foods!

PROJECTION (text):
Dr. Vandana Shiva, director of the Research Foundation for Science, Technology, and Ecology, Delhi, India

They have been found by Dr. Árpád Pusztai [*pronounced "Poosh-tai"*] of the Rowett Institute of Great Britain to have a negative impact on the immune systems of rats, and yet the entire regulation of GM foods in the world is based on the presumption of "substantial equivalence." Indeed, we do not have any system for looking at unique impacts of GM foods, because it is assumed they are the same, and therefore you don't *see* the difference, and you don't look for the difference and therefore you say you haven't found anything different. It's a "don't look, don't see" strategy, by which large acreages have been put under genetically engineered foods, and people have usually in ignorance been consuming them!

SISTER CATHERINE:

Dear Mr. Mansbridge, I am *urging you* to do a story on the *National* to make Canadians more aware of Percy Schmeiser's story.

SHIVA:

We have the privilege today to give the Navdanya Award to someone who has, over the past few years, dealt with the most oppressive impact of an intellectual property regime over seeds. I would like to invite one of our very eminent organic farmers ...

An OLD INDIAN FARMER dressed in a white dhoti enters.

... to give the Navdanya Award for the *defence* of seed sovereignty to Percy Schmeiser of Canada.

The OLD INDIAN FARMER walks slowly across the stage to present PERCY with the Navdanya Award. The trophy is a statuette of Gandhi. As he walks:

SISTER CATHERINE:
To Bob Cox, national editor at the *Globe and Mail*, Percy Schmeiser is a hero of the people! He was in India recently where he was awarded ...

The OLD INDIAN FARMER reaches PERCY finally and gives him the award.

OLD INDIAN FARMER:
The Navdanya Award.

PERCY:
Thank you very much. I'm really deeply, deeply honoured to have this privilege bestowed upon me.

Pause.

Today I attended a memorial for Mahatma Gandhi on his one hundred and thirty-first birthday, and it was a very moving experience, because I saw how he fought against the suppression of the people of India. We are now having that same suppression of farmers around the world in the control of the seed supply by multinational corporations. You must fight and fight *hard* to always maintain the seeds of food, which are the seeds of life. And I say to the people of India, if you don't resist, you will be under the domination of multinationals. Thank you very much.

Applause.

PERCY poses for photos with his statuette of Gandhi. ZITA MAIER, a reporter for the Prairie Messenger *in Saskatchewan, sees the photo of PERCY with his Gandhi statuette and reports the news in Canada.*

MAIER:

Percy Schmeiser's ongoing fight for farmers to keep their right to use their own seed has brought him something he didn't expect:

PLAYWRIGHT:

Zita Maier, reporter for the *Prairie Messenger* in Saskatchewan.

MAIER:

India's Mahatma Gandhi Award.

PERCY:

(*speaking to reporters after his speech*) The Mahatma Gandhi Award.

MAIER:

The award is given by Gandhi's family for the betterment of humankind.

PLAYWRIGHT:

Um ... the award was not given by Gandhi's family and was not called the Mahatma Gandhi Award – it was a statuette of Gandhi, but it was called the *Navdanya Award*.

PERCY:

Life-giving form is such a sacred thing. They're messing with something *God* created.

MAIER:

Schmeiser was not only honoured by receiving the Mahatma Gandhi Award, but the day was also an emotional one, he said, because it was his forty-eighth wedding anniversary, and it was the first time in their marriage he and his wife, Louise, were not together for the occasion.

> *LOUISE, at home, watches the TV news reports of PERCY's experience in India.*

SCENE 5

*The PLAYWRIGHT is working late at night at her kitchen
table in Montreal, at this point beginning to assemble her
interview footage into a play. Her husband enters with a
box of digital tapes and a baby bottle.*

HUSBAND:
   Look what I found.

   He drops the box on the table.

PLAYWRIGHT:
   Oh my God, where was it?

HUSBAND:
   In the dirty laundry hamper in her room.

PLAYWRIGHT:
   Shit, I'm really losing it ... oh thank goodness, here it is, the last
   interview with Percy.

HUSBAND:
   You're welcome.

PLAYWRIGHT:
   I love you.

HUSBAND:
   (*opening the fridge to put away the baby bottle*) Your daughter
   wants a goodnight hug.

PLAYWRIGHT:
   She's still awake?

HUSBAND:
   Yeah, she's doing that exhausted whining thing again.

PLAYWRIGHT:

She's fine. She has to learn to fall asleep by herself. I just gotta get through this section.

HUSBAND:

How's it going?

PLAYWRIGHT:

Agh ... I'm stuck. I have this character ... you know ... Vandana Shiva ... she's so great. She's saying that GM food is potentially harmful to human health but I can't find any science ... you know, any peer-reviewed science to back it up. Every website that talks about GM food is kind of granola, grassroots, under-funded ... you know the type. So, do I keep her voice in the play without backing up what she's saying?

SHIVA:

GM food is not equivalent to non-GM food.

PLAYWRIGHT:

I may have to do a follow-up interview with Ann Clark in Guelph.

HUSBAND:

You're leaving again? When?

PLAYWRIGHT:

I don't know, maybe Thursday?

HUSBAND:

I have a callback for that Petro-Canada ad on Thursday.

PLAYWRIGHT:

My mum can help out ...

HUSBAND:

Do we have any beer?

PLAYWRIGHT:
Uh, yeah, it's on the bottom shelf behind the carrot juice. Can
you pass me the yoghurt?

HUSBAND:
We finished it at lunch. I'll get some tomorrow.

PLAYWRIGHT:
I'm having a craving.

HUSBAND:
I'm having a beer.

He pops the top off his beer bottle.

PLAYWRIGHT:
So nice to have a drink anytime you want one.

HUSBAND:
Oh, come on ... it's minus 20 outside.

PLAYWRIGHT:
Wow. She just kicked. You wanna come feel?

HUSBAND touches her tummy and reacts to a big kick.

See? She wants yoghurt with honey.

*HUSBAND puts down his beer and walks toward the front
door to go buy the yoghurt.*

Thank you. Can you get the organic plain one?

HUSBAND:
I'm not spending twenty-five bucks on yoghurt.

PLAYWRIGHT:
It's worth it.

HUSBAND:
Go see your daughter. She's crying for you.

HUSBAND exits.

SCENE 6

The PLAYWRIGHT in interview with DR. ANN CLARK.

CLARK:

I'm willing to stand up and get crucified on this. I'm fifty-two years old and I'm only an associate professor. I'm not a high flyer in research. I'm not a molecular geneticist. But I have a young family, and I am very anxious to not make a mistake in what I feed my son, so I take this very personally as a mother.

PLAYWRIGHT:

So, you think there is something fundamentally flawed with the science of GM food ... the *safety* of GM food?

CLARK:

Well, I don't know. But we are definitely pushing ahead with this technology *way* before the science is there.

PLAYWRIGHT:

How so?

CLARK:

Well, the whole premise of genetic engineering is that you can snip out a particular gene and put it in a new host, and that the inserted gene is going to behave in a *predictable* way – it's going to transfer a trait, like herbicide tolerance, from one species to another, and it's going to do this in a *precise* way.

SHIVA:

But it is *not* precise!

CLARK:

Well, it turns out that it is not precise. Genetic modification is a very elegant technology up to the point of snipping out the gene ... but then when you put it in a new host, it goes in randomly.

ALTOSAAR:

And Ann Clark knows this because she studies pasture production systems?

CLARK:

They have no control of where it's going to land in the new host. They don't know which chromosome it's going to go on. They don't know where it's gonna go *on* the chromosome.

SHIVA:

And they don't know how it's going to affect other living organisms.

CLARK:

Which meant nothing to me until I did some more reading. And it turns out that where the new gene lands matters, because where it lands influences the expression of other unrelated genes – genes that have nothing to do with the trait in question.

PLAYWRIGHT:

But is there any conclusive proof that this modification process will produce organisms that are dangerous to ingest?

CLARK:

Well, in general, the science is lagging behind.

SHIVA:

The science is non-existent because it's not being funded.

ALTOSAAR:

It's not being funded because it's *junk science.*

CLARK:

But some research about the unintended consequences of GM technology is starting to get into the refereed literature.

PLAYWRIGHT:

What do you mean exactly by "unintended consequences"?

CLARK:
Well, to be honest, I don't know enough to get really substantive about this.

ALTOSAAR:
That's the understatement of the century.

PLAYWRIGHT:
Do you know anyone else who can?

ALTOSAAR:
Just come to my lab and speak to my grad students.

SHIVA:
She should go see Barry Commoner in the U.S. ...

CLARK:
You could go see Barry Commoner in the U.S.

PLAYWRIGHT:
Who?

CLARK:
Barry Commoner. He's a classical old-time ecologist at Queen's College in New York.

ALTOSAAR:
"Old" being the operative word.

CLARK:
He's been questioning the Watson-Crick theory of DNA for a long time. His theory is that the gene is only half the story inside the cell. Here, read this.

> CLARK hands the PLAYWRIGHT an article by DR. BARRY
> COMMONER: "Unraveling the DNA Myth: The Spurious
> Foundation of Genetic Engineering."

It'll blow your mind.

PLAYWRIGHT:

(*reading*) "In a genetically modified plant, the harmonious interdependence of the alien gene and the new host's protein system is likely to be disrupted in unpredictable ways. The genetically engineered crops now being grown all over the world represent a massive, uncontrolled experiment whose outcome is inherently unpredictable. The results could be catastrophic."*

The PLAYWRIGHT composes an email to COMMONER.

Dear Dr. Commoner, I have some questions relating to the science of genetic modification that I would like to ask you in person. Can I please schedule an interview with you in New York as soon as possible?

Commoner's article, which was published in the February 2002 issue of Harper's, *has been edited here for the stage.*

SCENE 7

PLAYWRIGHT in interview with JORDAN.

JORDAN:

Excuse me, but for most consumers, if you ask, "What's your number-one food safety concern?" *Unprompted?* Biotech doesn't even get mentioned till about nine or ten.

PLAYWRIGHT:

But you didn't even tell the public when you introduced these products ... and even today we are not allowed to label GM products.

JORDAN:

Well, labelling is *not* Monsanto's responsibility.

PLAYWRIGHT:

But my point is, the public doesn't know *when* they are consuming them. Why didn't you ask the public their opinion?

JORDAN:

Why the hell would you talk to consumers?! We didn't even think it would be an *issue.*

PLAYWRIGHT:

But *why not*? Why would you just assume that?

JORDAN:

Because GM food is *substantially equivalent* to non-GM food!

SHIVA:

No, it's not; that is the lie that industry and governments have fed to the public.

JORDAN:

No, I'm sorry ... you don't get regulatory approval in Canada unless you *prove* it's substantially equivalent.

CLARK:

But our "regulatory process" is not *regulating*; it's facilitating entry into the marketplace!

ALTOSAAR:

Okay, you have a daughter, correct? So, your daughter's sick. "Doctor, please! Use anything you have to save my daughter!"

SHIVA:

The biotech industry says these products are "exactly like nature made them ..."

ALTOSAAR:

"Well, it involves recombinant genetics and we don't know the long-term effects."

SHIVA:

... but when it comes to claiming property rights, they say, "We've made something novel."

ALTOSAAR:

"I don't give a shit! Save my daughter!"

SHIVA:

Now, I call this "ontological schizophrenia."

ALTOSAAR:

But now you're worried because your daughter eats this GM canola oil?

JORDAN:

Listen. Just *listen*. When Monsanto was developing these products, it was a company filled with brilliant scientists and their customers were *farmers*.

PLAYWRIGHT:
But did Monsanto even explain the science of genetic modification to the *farmers*?

JORDAN:
Of course we did.

CLARK:
No, they didn't!

PLAYWRIGHT:
The farmers understood the concept of *gene transfer* between different species?

JORDAN:
Well, they're *farmers*, not research scientists!

SHIVA:
Except now farmers *have* to understand genetics or they'll be sued!

ALTOSAAR:
Oh, *God*!

JORDAN:
They know they can spray their crop with Roundup and it ain't gonna die.

NADÈGE:
Oh, Monsanto will say, "We did this because we want to help farmers ..."

JORDAN:
And the farmer's thinking, "Holy cow! This is amazing!"

NADÈGE:
Well, the farmers I've spoken to couldn't be more adamant that they don't want it.

JORDAN:

But this is *my* perception of what farmers were probably thinking.

PLAYWRIGHT:

But what if the farmer is unaware that the science behind the product has not been proven to be 100 percent safe?

JORDAN:

But science is never 100 percent safe.

CLARK:

I'm sorry, but in Europe this technology has been *banned* until further testing is done.

ALTOSAAR:

Well, *I'm* sorry, but in *Europe*, they buy genetically engineered insulin and they inject themselves every day.

CLARK:

But I bet they've tested that process.

ALTOSAAR:

And it's even *pig*! Insulin is the *pig gene* put into a *yeast*!

JORDAN:

You can't do a test that is 100 percent perfect!

CLARK:

I'm not saying 100 percent ...

NADÈGE:

Once upon a time, we did research because it was about science for the public good.

SHIVA:

Hear! Hear!

NADÈGE:
Now we have scientists in labs trying to increase their profit margin.

ALTOSAAR:
Oh, but then you go to the store and you buy your soybean and you say, "Oh my God! It's got a gene in it!" (*bleats like a sheep*) That's *baaaaad.*

NADÈGE:
Look at the resumé of the company we're talking about: Monsanto!

ALTOSAAR:
"It's *baaaaad*!"

NADÈGE:
They brought us ...

SHIVA and NADÈGE:
... Agent Orange!

ALTOSAAR:
It may "flow," it may "gene."

SHIVA and NADÈGE:
Bovine growth hormone!

ALTOSAAR:
Who *owns* it?!

NADÈGE:
Whatever product they came up with, they leave a trail of dead people behind them!

ALTOSAAR:
Patents?! (*acting frightened*) Ahhh!

JORDAN:
We can't wait around testing everything until we know it's 100 percent safe! If ... if we *wait*, we're never going to have anything!

SHIVA:
Do you want *this company* to own the seeds of life?

JORDAN:
(*picking up PLAYWRIGHT's recording device*) You wouldn't have that thing. We wouldn't have a *microwave oven* or a car! You would have *nothing*!

Pause.

But the point is ... What are we even talking about?! That's not what this case is even about!

Pause.

All exit except JORDAN and PLAYWRIGHT.

Mr. Schmeiser told this little story at the trial and now every excuse in the book has come out since then: "Oh, well, now this isn't just about me; this is about saved seed and the *safety* of GMOs and this is about patents and ... and who controls life!"

I mean, none of this has anything to do with the case! Oh, but I gotta give him credit though. He got caught with his hand in the cookie jar and now he's got hundreds of thousands of activists supporting him all over the world. I mean, he's having a *great* time! He's a big celebrity! Good for him!

PLAYWRIGHT:
That must be slightly irritating for you.

JORDAN:
Well, no, not *irritating* ... I'm not *irritated*. I am just ... just *surprised* at how many people are being duped.

PLAYWRIGHT:
You say he got caught with his hand in the cookie jar, but no one has actually proven he stole your seeds.

JORDAN:
Look: we still believe that Mr. Schmeiser obtained this seed inappropriately.

PLAYWRIGHT:
From who?

JORDAN:
From somebody. From another grower who was contracted to use it.

PLAYWRIGHT:
Why can't you just find that person to corroborate your allegation?

JORDAN:
Well, because, first of all, that's *illegal* what that person did, so that person would be implicating themselves, okay? And the second thing, okay?

   Pause.

Listen: I have a master's degree in communication and my undergraduate degree was partially in journalism. When I was goin' to school ... and I'm old now ... so when I think back to, you know, that idealistic viewpoint that you had of ... of ... of fighting to find the *truth* in a story ... there's been *no* investigative journalism that's gone on in this case at all! And I know *why* media don't examine Mr. Schmeiser's story closely, you know, and ask him tough questions, and ask him to substantiate his stories – because they're trying to sell newspapers.

PLAYWRIGHT:
I'm not trying to sell anything.

JORDAN:
Well then, my dear, I think you have some more work to do.

   JORDAN exits.

PLAYWRIGHT:
Trish Jordan had avoided most of my questions about the science of GM food, but she was right about one thing. I hadn't spoken to anyone from the Saskatchewan farm community except Percy so far.

Sound of an airplane flying overhead.

SCENE 8

*PLAYWRIGHT interviews JEFF HOINESS, representative
of the Canadian Canola Growers Association in Saskatoon.*

HOINESS:

Let me put it to you this way: 99 percent of the canola grown in
Saskatchewan is genetically modified canola, so I would argue
that we producers have spoken with our wallets.

PLAYWRIGHT:

Do you remember how GM canola was introduced to you by
companies like Monsanto back in 1996?

HOINESS:

I don't remember. For me, I think it was introduced more as a
system to deal with weed control.

PLAYWRIGHT:

But were you told that the seed was genetically modified?

HOINESS:

Don't remember. But, see, back then there wasn't the big ... there
wasn't the publicity then that there is today.

PLAYWRIGHT:

But doesn't it seem important to you that the seed is genetically
modified?

HOINESS:

Not really. I mean, I have a great deal of trust in our regulatory
system. It wouldn't be introduced to the public unless there were
assurances that it was safe.

PLAYWRIGHT:

So, why didn't the government tell the public that GM seeds
were being introduced if they were so sure they were safe?

HOINESS:

I don't know ... that'd be a good question for the Canadian government, I would think.

PLAYWRIGHT:

So, the fact that Percy has brought all this public awareness to the issue of GM crops, you don't see that as a good thing, then?

HOINESS:

Not really. I mean, as a canola producer, I have a lot to lose if everyone starts challenging Monsanto. GM canola has made us way more money than we made before.

PLAYWRIGHT:

But your organization represents *all* canola growers. So, if Percy was a conventional grower and then GM seed ended up growing in his fields ... don't you see that as a problem for farmers who want to grow conventional canola?

HOINESS:

Percy Schmeiser has been found guilty in court. So, I think that his specific legal case is beyond our organization to comment on.

PLAYWRIGHT:

Do you have any personal opinions about it though?

Pause.

HOINESS:

Well, as a professional farmer and a farmer with a bachelor of science in agriculture (and a lot of experience), I don't believe a word he says in terms of how the canola got on his land.

PLAYWRIGHT:

Why don't you believe him?

HOINESS:

Because it's my understanding that it ended up on one thousand acres of his farm, basically corner to corner.

PLAYWRIGHT:
The 1998 crop, you mean?

HOINESS:
I believe so. Do I believe that some of it could have blown off a truck and ended up in his field? To get that much seed, to seed one thousand acres, you would need five thousand pounds of seed. Five thousand pounds is a lot of seed. It comes in fifty-pound bags; that's one hundred bags of seed.

PLAYWRIGHT:
I don't think Percy argued that so much seed fell off a truck in the first year ...

HOINESS:
Listen: I know that Percy's been successful over the years, and you don't become successful over the years by growing bad crops. But we have a neighbour who is originally from Bruno, and she ... Well, anyway, in that area in Bruno, they just don't trust him.

SCENE 9

PROJECTION *(text):*
Bruno, Saskatchewan. Population: 495

The PLAYWRIGHT thinks for a moment and then takes out her cellphone and dials a number.

CARLYLE MORITZ is working in a field. A phone is ringing at his house. MORITZ'S WIFE enters and answers it.

MORITZ'S WIFE:
  Hello?

PLAYWRIGHT:
  Hello, may I please speak to Carlyle Moritz?

MORITZ'S WIFE:
  Carlyle? Um, can I ask who's speaking?

PLAYWRIGHT:
  Home of Carlyle Moritz, Percy's farm assistant.

MORITZ'S WIFE:
  From Montreal, eh?

PLAYWRIGHT:
  I just arrived in Bruno and I'll be staying for a few days.

MORITZ'S WIFE:
  Oh, you're actually *in* town right now? Okay. Um ... let me just have a look see. Um ... I believe he actually just went out ... Can he call you later this evening?

PLAYWRIGHT:
  Um, sure. If you could just give him this phone number, that would be great.

MORITZ'S WIFE:
Okay then, I'll ask him to call you.

MORITZ'S WIFE goes out into the field to tell CARLYLE about the phone call.

The PLAYWRIGHT enters a hardware store, Main Street, Bruno, Saskatchewan. A twenty-something female SHOP CLERK is working there.

SHOP CLERK:
Can I help you?

PLAYWRIGHT:
Yes, thank you. Do you have any triple-A batteries?

SHOP CLERK:
I think we got some behind the counter here somewhere ...

Shift to PERCY making a speech about GMOs in Austin, Texas.

PERCY:
It's really a pleasure to come to Austin. I'd like to thank the organizers for bringing me here.

PLAYWRIGHT:
(*as she is paying for her batteries*) Um ... I'm just passing through town doing some research for a ... um ... a news article ... and was wondering if I could ask you some questions about Percy Schmesier and Monsanto's lawsuit against him.

SHOP CLERK:
Oh, I know nothing about it.

PLAYWRIGHT:
You must have heard about the case though.

SHOP CLERK:
Yes, I've *heard*, but I don't *know*.

PERCY:

I've been farming for fifty-three years. But besides being a farmer, I've also spent twenty-five years in public life. I was a Member of Parliament and I was also mayor of my community.

PLAYWRIGHT:

How about Percy? What do you know about him?

SHOP CLERK:

You're not quoting me or anything ...?

PLAYWRIGHT:

No ... no, it's just a background thing ... totally anonymous.

PERCY:

And in those years of public life, I always fought for farmers' rights and laws that would benefit them.

SHOP CLERK:

Well, I've just heard he's an ass. (*nervous laugh*)
I've heard he's kind of a ... a *crook*, I don't know.

PERCY:

So, anyway, that gives you a brief background; now I'll go immediately to what happened to me.

PLAYWRIGHT:

Where have you heard that?

SHOP CLERK:

Oh, just from people. Just from a few people I know around town.

PLAYWRIGHT:

What else have you heard?

Johannesburg, South Africa. Percy is being interviewed by a JOHANNESBURG RADIO INTERVIEWER.

103

JOHANNESBURG RADIO INTERVIEWER:
> (*female, South African accent*) Welcome to Jo'burg, Mr. Schmeiser.
> I can't tell you what an honour it is to have you on our
> program ...

> > *PROJECTION (text):*
> > Radio interview, Johannesburg, South Africa

JOHANNESBURG RADIO INTERVIEWER:
> Mr. Schmeiser, can you explain to our listeners the rationale
> behind the Canadian trial judge's ruling?

PERCY:
> In the judge's decision, you violate Monsanto's patent if it blows
> on your field or gets on your field regardless how.

> > *The PLAYWRIGHT has wandered into a senior citizens'*
> > *café on Main Street. The place is empty except for two*
> > *retired farmers sitting at a table.*

RETIRED FARMER 1:
> Percy? Oh, he lies faster than a horse can run! (*laughs*)

JOHANNESBURG RADIO INTERVIEWER:
> But how is it, Mr. Schmeiser, that the judge could come to that
> conclusion?

PERCY:
> He ruled that patent law is over and above farmers' rights.

RETIRED FARMER 1:
> Yeah, he was always a smart-ass kid and he hasn't changed yet.

> > *RETIRED FARMER 2 laughs.*

JOHANNESBURG RADIO INTERVIEWER:
> So, your case that you were a seed saver and you absolutely
> didn't *want* contamination from GM crops had no weight in
> the court?

PERCY:
No, none whatsoever; he ruled on *patent law*, not on farmers' *rights*.

RETIRED FARMER 1:
We both went to school with him. He was always different, but then his dad was different, too. So, it's one of those things.

PERCY:
Now, that is just one judge's ruling, and I have decided to appeal that ruling.

PLAYWRIGHT:
So, what's your view of his case against Monsanto?

RETIRED FARMER 1:
Well, he got caught with his hand in the cookie jar.

RETIRED FARMER 2:
Cookie jar!

RETIRED FARMER 1:
And instead of doing like some other people – paid up and shut up – he keeps fighting.

JOHANNESBURG RADIO INTERVIEWER:
This has been a tough fight for you, Mr. Schmeiser. How has it changed your life?

PERCY:
Well, it is ... my life really *has* changed. I wanted to retire. I wanted to go fishing with my grandkids.

PLAYWRIGHT:
Why would he keep fighting?

RETIRED FARMER 1:
Well, because he loves controversy and he loves publicity and he's gettin' it all over the world.

PERCY:

And one thing that really bothers me is the stress that it's put on my wife, Louise. She has a high blood pressure problem, and this sure has not helped.

RETIRED FARMER 1:

Yeah, I think he's something like old Hitler was …

PERCY:

And what has really added to our problems is … is really the intimidation by Monsanto's police.

RETIRED FARMER 1:

Hitler claimed that if you'd make a lie big enough and tell it often enough, people would tend to believe you.

PERCY:

They will watch us for days at a time. They'll park outside of our home and watch us all day long. They do all this just to intimidate and harass us!

PLAYWRIGHT:

Ok … thank you for speaking with me.

PLAYWRIGHT leaves café. NIEBRUGGE enters.

PLAYWRIGHT in interview with NIEBRUGGE.

PLAYWRIGHT:

Mr. Niebrugge, I assume from your testimony at trial that you also believe Percy deliberately planted Monsanto's seed.

NIEBRUGGE:

Oh, I can tell you for a fact that he deliberately planted those seeds.

PLAYWRIGHT:

What? You can?

NIEBRUGGE:

Yeah, he bought them off one of the farmers in our town.

Pause.

PLAYWRIGHT:
How could you know that?

NIEBRUGGE:
Because I confronted him before the trial about it. Before the
trial started, I thought I better tell Percy how I felt about the
whole thing. So, I told him, "This is what I believed happened,
and this is what I'm going to say on the stand." And Percy was
wild as all hell, uhn? Like, he basically threatened me. He says:

PERCY:
You're going to be sorry!

NIEBRUGGE:
I said, "For what? Tellin' the truth?" About five minutes after I
talked to Percy, the guy that sold 'im the seed illegally comes to
visit me in Percy's truck. So, I know exactly where Percy went to
after he threatened me. The guy says to me, "I suppose you heard
that I … that I sold Percy the seed, huhn?" And I said, "Well, I'd
be lying if I told you I didn't hear that, eh?" And then he says,
"Yeah, I don't know why Percy's puttin' me through this; I could
lose my whole goddamned farm. Why didn't he just pay the
fifteen dollars an acre and shut up?"

PLAYWRIGHT:
But I don't understand … you know who Percy bought the seed
from … didn't you tell Monsanto that person's name?

NIEBRUGGE:
No. Monsanto knew that I didn't want to bring them down, so
they respected that and they never asked me those questions.

PLAYWRIGHT:
But that's all they needed to win the case! I'm sorry, but I find it
hard to believe that they wouldn't have pressed you for that
information.

NIEBRUGGE:
Well, because that farmer and his family … they were paying the
fifteen dollars an acre. And they're pretty decent people, and I

think Monsanto didn't wanna get them in trouble. You know that would give Monsanto a bad name, kind of, eh?

PLAYWRIGHT:
Give *Monsanto* a bad name?!

NIEBRUGGE:
Yeah.

> *Pause.*

You don't understand, do ya? *Percy's* the one with the bad reputation around here. Everybody here has a story about how he did something to their family.

PLAYWRIGHT:
(*reluctant*) Like what?

> *Transition begins into Scene 10.*
>
> *PERCY begins his speech to the Sierra Club in Vancouver in 2003.*

PERCY:
Before I was sued by Monsanto, I never had anything to do with their GM canola.

PLAYWRIGHT:
(*reacting as if the stories she has just heard are very incriminating about PERCY*) But why would Percy have to do things like that? He's well off, isn't he? He's such a successful farmer.

NIEBRUGGE:
No! He is the crappiest farmer around here! Everything that comes out of his mouth is a lie.

PERCY:
I never bought their seed.

PLAYWRIGHT:
Why should I believe you?

NIEBRUGGE:

Well, what would I get outta lying like that?

PLAYWRIGHT:

It was suggested in court that you had something to gain from Monsanto.

NIEBRUGGE:

Yeah, a leather jacket. Whippy-ding.

PERCY:

So, when we lost the trial, we went to the Federal Court of Appeal.

PLAYWRIGHT:

You were taken out ... by Monsanto ... to ... to the Brier ...

NIEBRUGGE:

Yeah, *curling*! The bigger fuel companies get taken by bus to hockey games in Edmonton.

PERCY:

All three appeal judges ruled against me.

PLAYWRIGHT:

But how could he fool so many people?

NIEBRUGGE:

Because it's so easy to get people on your side who don't like Monsanto.

PERCY:

But we still stood up to them. Because we felt that if farmers ever lose the right to use their own seed, the future development of new seeds and plants would be stopped.

PLAYWRIGHT:

Would you be willing to give me the name and phone number of the farmer who sold Percy the seed?

NIEBRUGGE writes the phone number down on the back of a matchbook. The PLAYWRIGHT holds the matchbook in her hand as PERCY continues to speak.

SCENE 10

PERCY appeals directly to the live audience in the theatre.

PERCY:
And so my wife, Louise, and I decided to take our case to the Supreme Court of Canada. And tonight I'd like to explain the main issues of what the supreme court will be addressing.

PROJECTION (text):
Percy's speech to the Sierra Club, Vancouver, 2003

Can living organisms, seeds, plants, genes, and human organs be owned and protected by corporate patents on intellectual property? Can farmers' rights to grow conventional or organic crops be protected? Can farmers keep the ancient right to save their own seed? Who owns life?

Now, one issue that you *never* hear about with GMOs is the issue of corporate control of contracts that exist on the prairies of North America. To me, Monsanto's TUA – technology user agreement – is one of the most vicious contracts on the face of the earth, taking farmers' rights away. These are some of the main points in a contract with Monsanto: A farmer can never use his own seeds. You must always buy seeds from Monsanto. You must only buy your chemicals from Monsanto. If you commit some violation of this contract, and they fine you, you must sign a non-disclosure statement that you cannot talk to the media or to your neighbours about what Monsanto has done to you. You must pay Monsanto a licence fee of fifteen dollars an acre per year for the privilege of growing their seeds. You must permit Monsanto's detectives to come onto your land or look in your granaries for three years after you sign this contract, even though you may only grow it one year.

And who are Monsanto's police force? Former RCMP officers. And they always say they're ex-RCMP, and a lot of the time the farmer never hears the "ex," he only hears "police."

Now, what do you think happens when these gene police come into a farmer's home? The farmer will wonder which neighbour caused him the trouble. So, now we have the breakdown of farmers not trusting one another and afraid to talk to one another. We have the breakdown of our rural farm culture and society where farmers are not working together or trusting one another. This is one of the worst things that can happen.

I get asked a lot why farmers ever started to grow GMOs when they were introduced in 1996. At that time, Monsanto told farmers, among other things, that GMOs would give us bigger yields. But the U.S. Department of Agriculture has admitted that soybean yield is down at least 15 percent since 1996. Monsanto has said, "We'll now be able to feed a hungry world." But I say that feeding a hungry world doesn't take the Monsantos of this world. What it takes to feed a hungry world is *farmers*!

Now, remember there is no such thing as containment with GMOs. You can't have GMOs in the country and have organic or conventional farmers. It will all eventually be GMOs.

When I speak to farmers in Third World countries – Africa, India, Bangladesh – I tell them at least they have a choice left. We don't have a choice left for many of our grains in Canada. They're all contaminated. And we didn't have anybody to come and tell us what could happen. We believed Monsanto, but worst of all we believed our own federal government and they let us down with the introduction of GMOs. They were developed in government agricultural research stations across the Prairies without our consent, so Ottawa is fully responsible.

And I haven't even touched on the economic issue! We as Canadians cannot sell one bushel of canola to the EU because it's banned there! So, one-third of our markets have gone and our prices have dropped. Now they want to introduce GM wheat when even the Canadian Wheat Board said we would lose more than 80 percent of our market. That's how serious this is!

We have the right to know what we're eating. In Japan, the Netherlands, Germany, Switzerland, and England, extensive testing has been done on GMO products and they are starting to get results suggesting that there are serious health and environmental risks. The Canadian Food Inspection Agency did not do *one* bit of testing.

As I said, this is what's happening in *North America*!

In conclusion, why did we stand up to Monsanto? My wife and I are seventy-two and seventy-three. We don't know how many good years we have left and we look at it this way: as a grandfather, I ask what kind of legacy I want to leave my grandchildren. My grandparents and parents left a legacy of land. I don't want to leave my children a legacy of land, air, and water full of poisons. I'm sure all of you tonight feel the same way.

PERCY leaves the podium and marches into the supreme court hearing scene. PERCY sits behind ZAKRESKI.

SCENE 11

The Supreme Court of Canada, January 2004.

ZAKRESKI:
Madam Chief Justice McLachlin and members of the court ...

PLAYWRIGHT:
The supreme court hearing of Percy Schmeiser and Schmeiser
Enterprises Ltd. v. Monsanto Canada Inc. and Monsanto
Company was presided over by all nine justices on
January 20, 2004.

ZAKRESKI:
This appeal is about scope of rights and, in particular, the scope
of rights between the holder of a patent and the rights of a
farmer. And our task here is to ascertain where to draw the line.

Where do Monsanto's rights stop and the farmer's begin?
First, there is no claim in Monsanto's patent to a plant. The
patent claims are limited to a gene and a cell. Now, the federal
courts below interpreted these claims in a very broad way. Not
only does Monsanto's patent apply to that first-created cell, that
progenitor cell that was created in the laboratory, but, the way
the courts interpreted it, it applied to all the other differentiated
cells down the road – all the billions of omegas that regenerated
from the alpha. And it was by doing that, that they were able to
find Mr. Schmeiser to be a patent infringer because Monsanto
detected patented genes in the leaf and seed cells of his canola.

Our contention is that if this is what the claims result in, if the
patent extends to every cell in the plant, then what you have
done indirectly is claimed protection for a plant. Because, to say
that you haven't claimed a plant when you've claimed every cell
within it, is to say that you haven't claimed Canada when you've
claimed every province, every territory, and every speck of dust
within it. And if that's what the patent claims mean, then our
contention is that this is a claim to unpatentable material.

HUGHES:

Chief justice and justices of this court. As I understand it, my
friend is making arguments based on what he infers should be a
different philosophical approach to reading the Patent Act and
we submit that this is not a forum for parliamentary
amendments to the Patent Act.

This case, we submit, is a rather simple case of patent
infringement. *Nine* fields, *1,038* acres of *95 to 98 percent* pure
Roundup Ready canola. Now, the canola plant itself is not
Monsanto's invention. The invention is this new gene. And the
invention is the *way* that the gene is inserted into the plant's
cell ...

JUSTICE BASTARACHE [PLAYWRIGHT]:

If you *had* patented the plant, what would be the difference
between what you would be claiming and what you're claiming
now?

HUGHES:

Because the whole plant is not my invention. My invention is
part of the plant – the gene and the cell.

JUSTICE ARBOUR [PLAYWRIGHT]:

But you say in your materials that "Schmeiser was aware that he
had the invention."

HUGHES:

Yes.

JUSTICE ARBOUR:

But the plant is not the invention.

HUGHES:

That's right.

JUSTICE ARBOUR:

So, in what way can we say that he had the *invention,* which is
the isolated cell in which the modified gene was implanted prior
to differentiation?

HUGHES:

Because he went out there and he sprayed it and 60 percent survived!

JUSTICE ARBOUR:

But you say the invention is not the plant. In what sense, in what legal or factual sense, can we say that Schmeiser had what was patent protected, which is the isolated cell prior to differentiation?

HUGHES:

No, no, I ... I am not using the word "isolated" here, Your Honour.

JUSTICE ARBOUR:

Maybe that is all the law entitles you to.

HUGHES:

The law entitles me to the cell because that's new! But once I have it, I don't just put it on the shelf as a laboratory curiosity. I go out and I *use* it! A claim to a gene sitting on the lab shelf is of no value. The purpose of the Patent Act is to encourage research and development. If you don't give protection for the infringement by using the plant, you will have a hollow Patent Act.

ZAKRESKI:

My Lords, there is a threat that is being made here: that unless Mr. Schmeiser loses, unless there is a victory given to Monsanto, companies like Monsanto are gonna pull up their stakes and go elsewhere. To me that is not an argument that should hold sway ...!

HUGHES:

My Lords, Mr. Schmeiser suggested that the seed came in by the wind or insects or trucks or falling off farm equipment or swaths blowing from the fields. But the trial judge said, "I am persuaded by evidence of Dr. Keith Downey ..."

The PLAYWRIGHT takes out the matchbook with the phone number NIEBRUGGE gave her. We hear a phone

*number being dialed and then the sound of a phone
ringing. The ringing gets louder and louder.*

NADÈGE:

No!

HUGHES:

"... that none of the suggested sources could reasonably
explain the concentration of Roundup Ready canola found on
Mr. Schmeiser's property."

NADÈGE:

He can't bring this up now. We are too far in now to ... to be
looking at that now ...

HUGHES:

We have the evidence of his hired hand, Carlyle Mortiz, talking
to the local gas station attendant ...

NADÈGE:

That's not what the supreme court was even looking at ...
whether or not his field hand told the gas station guy ...

HUGHES:

Wesley Niebrugge.

NADÈGE:

What kind of stupid idiot lawyer are *you* to try to bring this up
now?! You didn't establish any of this in the lower courts!

HUGHES:

That Mr. Schmeiser deliberately planted Roundup Ready canola
in his fields.

NADÈGE:

He *didn't steal the seeds*! And even if he did, it's irrelevant at this
point!

ZAKRESKI:

> (*angry now, speaking to PLAYWRIGHT*) Listen: if you think that he obtained the seed illegally, find me the person. Monsanto couldn't prove it ... using all the money that they had. They spent three-quarters of a million dollars at his trial, they had all the private investigators they wanted, they had all the lawyers and legal help they wanted, and they couldn't prove that Percy lied! So, if somebody out there thinks that they can ... go ahead and try!

> *The BRUNO FARMER and his WIFE enter and look at the ringing phone. The WIFE picks it up.*

BRUNO FARMER'S WIFE:

> Hello? (*pause*) Hello?

PLAYWRIGHT:

> Yes, hello ... I'm calling from Montreal ... just doing some research for a story ...

BRUNO FARMER'S WIFE:

> From Montreal? What do you want? What is this about?

PLAYWRIGHT:

> Um ... I was just wondering if I could just speak with you about Percy Schmeiser and his case against ...

BRUNO FARMER'S WIFE:

> Oh no. No, thank you.

PLAYWRIGHT:

> Do you think I could just speak with your husband for a moment?

BRUNO FARMER'S WIFE:

> Oh no ... he's busy. No, he can't talk ...

PLAYWRIGHT:

> I'd just like to ask him ...

BRUNO FARMER'S WIFE:
No ... no. We've got company here.

She hangs up.

Pause.

CHIEF JUSTICE McLACHLIN (PLAYWRIGHT):
Thank you very much. The court will reserve its decision on this appeal and the court stands adjourned.

Sound of gavel.

SCENE 12

PROJECTION (text):
Interview with Dr. Barry Commoner, Long Island, New York

PLAYWRIGHT:

The Watson-Crick central dogma ... why does it continue to steer genetic science, even now that many of its theories about DNA have been proven false?

COMMONER:

Because money has distorted the scientific process.

PLAYWRIGHT:

Can you elaborate?

COMMONER:

Well, how much time do you have?

He looks at his watch.

I have to be in Manhattan to see a play at eight o'clock.

PLAYWRIGHT:

(*smiles*) As much as we can squeeze in before that then.

COMMONER:

Well, I guess you can appreciate that almost the entire output of biology research today is being translated into private enterprise This is a *total transformation* that has taken place in the past fifty years. And it's a transformation that superficially seems to be economic. But it also involves cultural changes within the science.

PLAYWRIGHT:

Like what?

COMMONER:

Well, take the slogan "It's too good to be true." When Watson was interviewed by *Time* magazine a few years ago, when he finally admitted that some aspects of his theory went too far, he said, "It was simply too good *not* to be true." His whole attitude was, "This thing is so beautiful, so powerful that it has to be true." And this is now a *cultural belief* that the younger scientists have been brought up with.

PLAYWRIGHT:

What was it about the theory, though, that in your opinion was perceived to be so powerful?

COMMONER:

Its simplicity. We love simple stories. "A nucleotide sequence in DNA contains all the instructions to create a particular trait in living organisms." This one-to-one, linear proposition completely ignores the fantastic complexity of life inside the cell. You read my article?

PLAYWRIGHT:

Yes.

COMMONER:

So, then you realize how many other players there are inside the cell that perform *key roles* in transmitting DNA's code.

PLAYWWRIGHT:

(*looking at her notes*) Yes ... like ... like ... spliceosomes?

COMMONER:

Like spliceosomes ... very good. Like all the chaperone proteins that repair DNA when it makes mistakes in the replication process. These processes evolved naturally over thousands of years ... you can't just grab one of those molecules, DNA, and insert it into an alien species with a different protein environment.

PLAYWRIGHT:

And yet we *have* done that ... I mean, we have managed to modify organisms to behave the way we want them to behave ...

121

COMMONER:

Well, we think they're behaving the way we want them to ... but who knows? We have *no clue* what the unintended consequences might be. No one has done any real testing – it's too expensive.

PLAYWRIGHT:

Which brings us back to the problem of money.

COMMONER:

Yes. Even the few so-called public scientists who are left who *could* devote some time to this, they're not *questioning* the science of recombinant genetics because they're afraid – afraid of not getting tenure, afraid of not publishing, afraid of not getting the research dollars.

PLAYWRIGHT:

But what about the public? If they knew about this ... they could demand a change ... couldn't they?

COMMONER:

The public? Well, let me tell you ... I'm eighty-seven years old and I have devoted my career to trying to communicate science to the public. But too often scientists have dismissed the public as being incapable ... as being "irrational." The irony, of course, is that the biotechnology industry is based on science that is forty years old.

Pause. COMMONER looks at his watch.

Can we make this the last question now?

PLAYWRIGHT:

Of course. Um, James Watson declared that DNA's text would express the "ultimate description of life." What is your ultimate description of life?

COMMONER:

Life.

Pause.

Life is life. In other words, what is it that is self-replicating?
Is it protein? DNA? No. It's *life*. It's an *indivisible* entity. I mean,
you can break it apart, but it's not what it was before. And it's
true: how do we analyze the components of life? The first thing
we do is to kill the living thing, right?

PLAYWRIGHT:
Right.

SCENE 13

PERCY picks up his home phone and dials a number. The PLAYWRIGHT's cellphone rings. A LAB TECHNICIAN gives the PLAYWRIGHT a piece of paper; she reads from it before answering the phone.

PLAYWRIGHT:
May 21, 2004. The *Globe and Mail*. The Supreme Court of Canada made biotechnology history today with a 5–4 ruling in favour of ... Monsanto.

LAB TECHNICIAN 2:
The ruling is said to have profound implications for the global biotechnology industry, where genetic engineering has made inroads.

LAB TECHNICIAN 4:
In a personal victory for Schmeiser, however, the supreme court overturned a previous ruling demanding that he pay Monsanto's legal fees associated with the case.

LAB TECHNICIAN 5:
The court decided that Schmeiser earned no profit from Monsanto's invention and that the company is therefore entitled to nothing on their claim of account.

PLAYWRIGHT:
Hello?

PERCY:
Annabel, Percy Schmeiser in Saskatchewan calling.

PLAYWRIGHT:
Percy, how are you?

PERCY:

Yeah ... really good, thank you. How are you?

PLAYWRIGHT:

Fine, thank you.

PERCY:

No, the reason I'm calling is because I had a call this morning from some people in Bruno who said you were calling them last night and they were kind of concerned about some of the statements you had made. One of the comments, and I don't know if it's correct or not, is that you said I'm not well liked in my community. Did you make that statement?

PLAYWRIGHT:

Um ... well ...

PERCY:

Because I don't know if you know this, but since the trial, I've been elected as deputy mayor of our town. So, you know, you have to remember that Monsanto has come in here and has offered people money and product to say negative things about me.

LOUISE enters and listens to the conversation.

You know, and so now when people get a phone call from somebody in Montreal and says he's not well liked in the community, they kind of *resent that,* huhn?

PLAYWRIGHT:

Yes, I understand ...

PERCY:

The people who called me were actually surprised that you had their names and phone numbers, you know?

PLAYWRIGHT:

Yes, I can imagine that I must have seemed very intrusive.

PERCY:

They ask *me*, "What's goin' on? Why is this being dug up?" I mean, you can imagine how many phone calls they get from all over the world. And we don't know how many of these are put up by Monsanto. But people are just getting so tired of it. And I often feel bad – the situation I not only put my family into by standing up to Monsanto, but that my neighbours should be harassed or intimidated or get phone calls and get asked leading questions, huhn?

LOUISE takes the phone out of PERCY's hand.

PLAYWRIGHT:

I'm sorry.

LOUISE hangs up the phone.

EPILOGUE

PLAYWRIGHT:
The power of perception is infinite.

I know that for every one of you sitting in the audience tonight, there will be a different interpretation of this play. That is how it should be.

But for me there is one irrefutable truth about Percy: his resistance ignited a worldwide narrative about GM seeds that continues to sprawl in contradictory directions even today.

Right now in Brazil, five million farmers are fighting a class-action lawsuit against Monsanto to defend their right to save soybean seeds produced from Roundup Ready plants. On the other side of the planet, however, the Chinese government is considering the introduction of genetically modified rice as a means to sustain its 1.3 billion inhabitants.

The mystery at the heart of Percy's story remains troubling for me. But after my meeting with Barry Commoner, I choose to see that mystery as an eloquent expression of ... of the elusive, complex, and utterly uncontainable nature of life.

My fear, though, is that if we don't look for this ... this ... this ...

LAB TECHNICIAN 1:
This phenomenon?

PLAYWRIGHT:
This phenomenon ... yes, this *phenomenal* aspect of life, we won't see it. Because it's not that reality, or *biology*, or *life* has changed since Watson and Crick – it is our *perception* that is changing. It is *we* who must ask ourselves not just, "What is life?" but, "How do we want to see life modified?"

I think our future depends on it. But I am just one person.

The PLAYWRIGHT looks at the other actors onstage.

Not really.

Thank you for listening.

END

Annabel Soutar is the artistic director of Porte Parole, a Montreal theatre company dedicated to creating and producing original documentary plays about contemporary social and political issues. Her first play, *Novembre*, debuted in 2000. Since then she has written *2000 Questions* (2002) and contributed to *Sante!* (2003), a seven-part documentary series about Quebec's health care system. Her more recent docudrama, *Sexy béton (Sexy Concrete)* (2009/2010), explored the collapse of the de la Concorde overpass in 2006 and the culture of corruption in Quebec's construction industry. *Sexy béton* was named a finalist for the prestigious French playwriting award, Le Prix Michel-Tremblay, in 2011.